ILLEGAL

Also by Elizabeth F. Cohen

Semi-Citizenship in Democratic Politics

The Political Value of Time

Citizenship

ILLEGAL

HOW AMERICA'S LAWLESS IMMIGRATION
REGIME THREATENS US ALL

ELIZABETH F. COHEN

BASIC BOOKS
NEW YORK

Basic Books
Hachette Book Group
1290 Avenue of the Americas, New York, NY 10104
www.basicbooks.com

Printed in the United States of America
First Edition: January 2020

Published by Basic Books, an imprint of Perseus Books, LLC, a subsidiary of
Hachette Book Group, Inc. The Basic Books name and logo is a trademark of
the Hachette Book Group.

The publisher is not responsible for websites (or their content)
that are not owned by the publisher.

Print book interior design by Linda Mark.

Library of Congress Cataloging-in-Publication Data
Names: Cohen, Elizabeth F., 1973– author.
Title: Illegal: how America's lawless immigration regime threatens us all /
    Elizabeth F. Cohen.
Description: First edition. | New York: Basic Books, 2020. | Includes
    bibliographical references and index.
Identifiers: LCCN 2019039593 (print) | LCCN 2019039594 (ebook) | ISBN
    9781541699847 (hardcover) | ISBN 9781541699854 (ebook)
Subjects: LCSH: United States—Emigration and immigration—Government
    policy—History. | Emigration and immigration law—United States—History.
Classification: LCC JV6483 .C54 2020 (print) | LCC JV6483 (ebook) | DDC
    325.73—dc23
LC record available at https://lccn.loc.gov/2019039593
LC ebook record available at https://lccn.loc.gov/2019039594

LSC-C

10 9 8 7 6 5 4 3 2 1

For my mother,
Reggie Feiner Cohen.
You are our diamond: precious, radiant, strong, and bright.

Contents

Introduction

TO MANY WHO MAY BE DRAWN TO THIS BOOK, THE SADISTIC theatrics of Trump-era immigration policies have come as a shock. Images of families sleeping on gravel under a highway overpass, children in cages, and relatives separated by a racist Muslim ban contradict national self-understandings of the United States as a country of immigrants, or at least of humane laws. But this self-understanding never actually reflected the everyday experiences common to immigrants. The lives of most immigrants in the United States have often been marked by violence, cruelty, and exploitation. For a long time, social mobility dictated that those immigrants' children and grandchildren would never know how bad things were for their forebears, allowing all of us to view our history and ourselves through a rosy lens.

My own family—my mother, her sister, and their parents—arrived in the United States in 1950, after surviving the Holocaust and living for years in a displaced persons camp outside Vienna. Did they do things the "right way," as some people define it when distinguishing documented from undocumented immigrants? They had their papers—visas and clean bills of health. But their papers came by accident, as a matter of luck and persistence, not through a welcoming invitation to become American. They had evaded the numerous laws that were in place to keep as many immigrants like them as possible out of the country. Jews, Eastern Europeans especially, had not been welcome in the United States for a long time.

I carry with me everywhere the passport picture of my mother, Reggie, as a young child about to set foot on the boat that took them to the United States. In the photo, she sits, bright eyes shining, smiling, hands clasped in front of her with anticipation. She still adopts that expression today, when something we have long hoped for comes on the horizon. Going to America was the dream her family had nurtured as they made do in a refugee camp where they lived with other displaced families, separated only by sheets hung from the ceiling. She will also be the first to tell anyone who suggests otherwise that this country was and remains a disappointment. It wasn't just the cottony, flavorless loaves of supermarket bread, or the fact that Christmas, which is when they arrived, turned out to be the only time of the year when all the radio stations played beautiful classical music. The letdown had much deeper roots. My grandfather, Chaim, had longed for a formal education since he had been forced to leave school at age nine. But it wasn't possible to both go to school and work the grueling hours of backbreaking labor required to wrench the family out of insecurity and into the middle class. Worse, no one around him seemed to find this surprising or wrong. As a young man in Europe, in a brief moment of freedom, he had been drawn to discussions of socialist politics and theory. In the United States he could belong to a union, but there wasn't much socialism to be found, particularly of an intellectual variety. In the land of opportunity, most of the opportunity consisted of bosses and company owners helping themselves to the benefits afforded by immigrant labor, race privilege, and other forms of power.

In school, my mother observed among her peers the same lack of interest in education for education's sake. She applied to Union College, which wasn't yet accepting women, because it was inconceivable to her that she would not be allowed to attend. She was accepted, matriculated, and graduated, and then she faced even larger obstacles when she entered a PhD program where no one wanted to supervise women researchers. Each university she worked for was more corrupt than the last, and vulnerable people around her—immigrants, disabled people, and people who came to the Northeast from poorer, more rural places—were treated terribly, often in plain sight of others who could have helped but were indifferent or complicit.

To people who have been disappointed in our country for a long time, the Trump era is not a shock. They already knew that the United States is prone to nativism, sexism, and racism, and that among those who aren't nativist, sexist, and racist are people who prefer to believe myths about liberty and justice rather than see the country for what it is. To the cynics, "This is not who we are" is self-delusion. The United States is a country that had trafficked in chattel slaves but didn't repeal restrictions on immigration from African countries until 1965; a country that aggressively executed a genocide of indigenous people in order to expropriate their land; a country that admitted Chinese workers and then succumbed to a movement to drive them out; a country where employers felt comfortable telling the Irish they need not apply; a country that rounded up people of Japanese descent, took their possessions, and tried to repatriate them; a country that violently drove Mexican Americans off land that had not too long prior been forcibly taken from Mexico.

The Muslim ban; the rejection of refugees and asylum seekers; the ease with which people ask, "What will we get out of the deal if we let you come here?"—all of "this" is exactly who we are and who we have always been. Those of us who do not like "this" do not have to accept the past as prologue. But we have our work cut out for us if we want to reframe narratives about nonexistent border crises, illegality, and dangerous immigrants.

Illegal is just a small part of that larger project. Its chapters contain a narrative about modern nativism, much of which is predicated on the supposed illegality of people trying to enter the country. Undocumentedness itself is a status that we legislated into existence—and one we can also legislate right back out of existence. Because any rules about what is legal or illegal start with legislative action, I have worked hard in this book to show where there is a legislative path out of our current conundrum, in which it has become impossible for most people who want to immigrate legally to do so. Achieving a legislative consensus on any changes will be tremendously difficult. But we can take some comfort from the fact that, in the past, moments of extreme nativism have been followed by opportunities to undo the damage. Smart, persistent activism over a period of years can propel us away from "this" and toward the country we want to be.

CHAPTER ONE

Enforcement Gone Rogue

IT CAN BE VERY DIFFICULT TO PERCEIVE THE PRECISE POINT AT which a democracy unravels and becomes a police state. But if you lived near the US-Mexico border in Texas in 2018, your daily routine may already have forced you into contact with characteristic features of authoritarianism like checkpoints, fortifications, heavily armed police, and constant surveillance. To accommodate the terrain around the Rio Grande River, large segments of the border wall have been located well within the United States. This leaves students, workers, and anyone else who needs to get from one side of the wall to the other with the choice between traveling through checkpoints or compromised sections of wall. People going about their daily business might never leave the United States but must still cross a border because of where border fortifications have been situated. Property owners have to use remote controls to open gates just to reach parts of their own land that have been walled off. Above, the buzz of Predator B drones, Black Hawk helicopters carrying armed agents, and man-hunting radar are now as much a part of the soundscape as the wind rustling brush. Sometimes armed civilians with no legal authority at all—self-appointed citizen militia border patrols—profile and harass people who they decide are suspicious.

Meanwhile, near the northern border of the country, residents who need to travel by train or bus are likely to be detained while armed Border Patrol agents search the vehicle they're on and question passengers, regardless of whether they are crossing the border or even if they are particularly near it. Actually crossing the border is even more fraught. Many remember a time when they could take day trips to Canada and maybe flash a driver's license if they crossed at a checkpoint. Now everyone waits in long lines, sometimes for hours, to prove their right to exit and enter. At times people crossing the border are required to divulge sensitive biometric data that can later be shared with other agencies without their consent or even a warrant.[1] Once they cross, US Customs and Border Protection (CBP) agents, whose stated mission is to police the border, might continue surveilling them in Canada. CBP can even fire tear gas at civilians trying to claim asylum, or close a busy entry or exit point with no notice, making thousands of people's daily commute impossible.[2]

In the vast interior of the country, where CBP is a less prominent presence, Immigration and Customs Enforcement (ICE), in pursuit of deportable residents, has been reaching further and more aggressively into the daily lives of Americans. ICE performs the bulk of immigration enforcement work, which is increasingly brutal toward the immigrants it targets. ICE is also starting to encroach on the civil liberties of citizens. ICE's work includes identifying and seeking out undocumented immigrants, giving them notice that they are going to be deported, incarcerating them, and deporting them. Each year, ICE raids infiltrate more of our workplaces and disrupt a wider array of neighborhoods, schools, and communities in increasingly indiscriminate searches for undocumented immigrants. ICE has also pushed to establish a shockingly large network of prisons, both public and private, where detainees languish, often for months at a time. ICE agents, facilities, and activities become a more potent and visible part of US communities with every passing year. ICE also gathers data to surveil citizens' political beliefs and activities—including protest actions they have taken on issues as far afield as gun control—in addition to immigrants' rights.

Slowly, sometimes even imperceptibly, the United States is becoming a fortress encased in steel and razor wire, guarded by dogs and a heavily armed paramilitary force. ICE and CBP form the heart of a broken immigration enforcement system that is gradually eroding the rights not only of noncitizens but of US citizens. So egregious have been their oversteps that an "Abolish ICE" movement gained surprising traction in 2018.

CBP escaped hashtag status even as it engaged in abuses easily as reprehensible as those conducted by ICE, eventually becoming infamous for agents joining secret racist Facebook groups and committing gross human rights violations against people in its custody.[3] In fact, ICE frequently is blamed for actions that were actually taken by CBP. (People's confusion is understandable: prior to 2003, one agency, the Immigration and Naturalization Service, oversaw both border control and interior enforcement.) And it was CBP agents that Donald Trump reportedly ordered to illegally deny entry to possible asylum seekers, promising the agents pardons if they did so.[4] It is a distraction to worry about which is worse when both are demonstrably dangerous. ICE and CBP are two arms attached to one body that is working on the same task: immigration security. But immigration laws are enforced amid an institutional culture of abuse and impunity.

Together, ICE and CBP form a sprawling law-enforcement apparatus in search of a justification for its own size and scope. The undocumented immigrant population in the United States stopped growing in 2007 and has declined since then by 13 percent.[5] The number of people arrested for entering the country without a valid visa or without an inspection by a United States Citizenship and Immigration Services (USCIS) agent, as opposed to overstaying a visa, is as low as it has been since 1972; enforcement methods had little to do with that fact. Some even advise that harsh enforcement and border fortifications serve to trap people inside the United States who would prefer to move back and forth over the border.

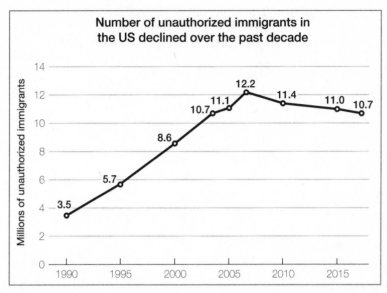

Number of unauthorized immigrants in the United States, 1990–2016. *Source:* Jeffrey S. Passel and D'Vera Cohn, "U.S. Unauthorized Immigrant Total Dips to Lowest Level in a Decade," Pew Research Center, November 27, 2018, https://www.pewhispanic.org/2018/11/27/u-s-unauthorized-immigrant-total-dips-to-lowest-level-in-a-decade/.

Data from Pew Hispanic Center, Center for Migration Studies, Mexican Migration Project, and Department of Homeland Security (DHS) all show the downward trend in undocumented immigration. The decline started around 2000 and picked up momentum in 2008, during the Great Recession. Levels have been dropping or have plateaued since then. The trend developed as increasing numbers of undocumented immigrants began leaving the country each year just as inflows fell. It is easy to forget this when anxiety about a periodic spike reaches a fever pitch. Observe CBP's own data estimating undetected unlawful entries over time:

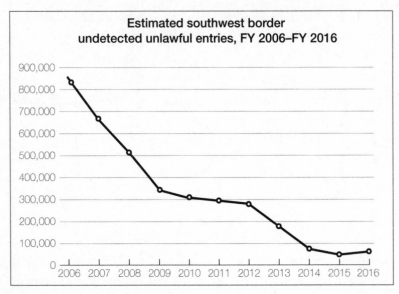

Estimated unlawful entries at the southwest border, 2006–2016. *Source:* US Department of Homeland Security, "Department of Homeland Security Border Security Metrics Report," May 2, 2018, p. 13, https://www.dhs.gov/sites/default/files/publications/BSMR_OIS_2016.pdf.

It is worth noting that this decline is not due to any immigration enforcement policies but derives from changes in the economies and societies of immigrant-sending countries. (Migration is highly age dependent—you're more likely to migrate out of a country when you are in your early twenties than when you're thirty—and Mexico, for example, has become an aging society, with an average age that has risen from 16.6 in 1970 to 28.6 in 2018.)[6] Not only have these changes drastically reduced the likelihood of Mexicans migrating to the United States without authorization; more undocumented migrants from Mexico are now leaving the United States than entering it. If there are increases in the future, those, too, will be driven by circumstances in the sending countries rather than by a failure to aggressively enforce immigration laws. Furthermore, the low and declining birthrates of native-born Americans caution against discouraging immigration as the population ages and requires younger workers to support older retirees.[7]

Crises can be manufactured—for example, when asylum seekers are prevented from presenting themselves at the border to request asylum, thus creating confusion, fear, and chaos on the Mexican side of the border. But those are humanitarian crises for the families seeking shelter, not security crises for the United States. Even when we include recent spikes in asylum-seeking, it remains the case that undocumented immigrants are not coming to the United States in nearly the numbers that they were in the 1990s and early 2000s. The bigger immigration picture is one in which the need for enforcement is shrinking even as expenditures on enforcement are rising. Often this wasteful spending comes at the expense of measures to process backlogs of asylum claims, visa applications, and even naturalization paperwork.

In fact, undocumented immigrants do not pose a grave danger to anyone, they do not deprive US citizens of jobs, and they do not burden the collective resources of the country. Overall, violent crime rates decline as immigration rises.[8] Not only do US citizens commit crimes at higher rates than immigrants,[9] but the only infraction most undocumented immigrants are guilty of is the federal misdemeanor of undocumented entry—a

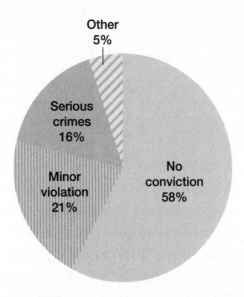

Conviction record of ICE detainees as of June 2018. *Source:* TRAC Immigration, "Profiling Who ICE Detains—Few Committed Any Crime," TRAC Research Center Report, October 9, 2018, https://trac.syr.edu/immigration/reports/530/.

violation they committed in large part because the US government has gone to great lengths to foreclose legal ways to enter or reside in the country. The majority of ICE detainees do not have a criminal record, and four-fifths of all ICE detainees have nothing more than a minor offense such as a traffic violation on their record.[10] Of those with a serious "level 1" offense on their record, a large proportion is for infractions like possession of small amounts of marijuana, which isn't even a crime in all states. Some studies show that using borders to combat drug trafficking can actually rebound, causing new, more dangerous drugs to appear.[11]

In the realm of employment, the presence of immigrants arguably has been stabilizing in recent years; immigrants do not suppress wages, and when immigrants—even undocumented ones—are not in the labor pool, companies tend to automate rather than hire, causing job markets to contract.[12] Further, undocumented immigrants actually subsidize US social programs, because a substantial proportion (around 40 percent) pays income taxes, contributing to programs like Medicaid, Medicare, and Social Security even though they are ineligible to draw on those programs.[13] Overall, many calculate that the tax contributions of immigrants exceed the costs associated with their presence, though some states bear more costs than others.[14]

You would never know any of this from the way we behave on our borders or from the way we treat our country's undocumented population. Public policies are supposed to be made rationally, and public resources are supposed to be used wisely, in accordance with the wishes and the interests of the public as well as the larger principles to which the country is committed. But when it comes to current immigration policy, neither prudence nor democratic will guides our policies.

Of course, given the armed-police presence and military-style fortifications being used to guard against the supposedly dire threat of undocumented immigrants infiltrating the country, it is unsurprising that some people have been persuaded that the undocumented immigrants already living in US communities pose a grave danger. For decades, nativist and white nationalist campaigns have worked to convince the public and its elected officials that undocumented immigrants are hardened criminals who take jobs away from US citizens and drain resources from social programs.[15] These anti-immigrant activists want us to believe that muscular enforcement practices will return law and order to an out-of-control country. They make the intuitive but almost entirely false argument that those entering and residing in the country without authorization are gangsters, rapists, and freeloaders, upending law and order and sucking up resources, and that we ought to remove them from our midst by any means necessary. Both anti-immigrant activists and a sizable number of ordinary citizens believe that brutally harsh enforcement is the best possible course of action when people are in the country without papers. A few may even think that undocumented immigrants should not have any rights at all.

At the urging of these activist lobbies and some prominent elected officials, our government has poured billions of dollars into policing the border and the interior of the country while searching for people to question, detain, and deport. This campaign was not triggered by Donald Trump, or even by post-9/11 security concerns. It is the product of a long-term policymaking endeavor that has deep roots in the origins of US federal immigration enforcement and that has been shaped by a few powerful elite groups with a white nationalist agenda. We'll examine these efforts in detail in the pages ahead.

In fact, it is our enforcement agencies, and not undocumented immigrants, who are flouting the law and soaking up more than their fair share of resources. These agencies and the private companies who receive contracts from them have amassed enormous budgets and accrued immense powers with disturbingly little oversight or accountability. Just think: the budget for ICE—only one of the three divisions of DHS devoted to the administration and enforcement of US immigration policy—is now ten times larger than the budget for the entire Immigration and Naturalization Service agency back in 1993, when undocumented immigration really was on the rise and national security had come into sharp focus as a justification for harsh enforcement. Even before the Trump buildup, in the middle of the Obama administration, Congress appropriated $18 billion for immigration enforcement—$4 billion more than it did *for all other federal criminal law-enforcement agencies combined.*[16] CBP is the country's largest law-enforcement organization—larger than the FBI, DEA, and all other federal enforcement agencies. Slowly and quietly, DHS and its subsidiary agencies—particularly ICE and CBP—have gained access to military-grade weapons, sprawling prison complexes, an army of field officers, and, critically, exemptions from some of the supervision that is supposed to keep law-enforcement officers from going rogue. What these agencies are doing with their power, often quite secretively, is sinister. Under the rationale that tolerating undocumented immigrants sabotages the rule of law, they routinely behave in ways that bespeak an utter indifference to the law and the rights it protects.

Many US citizens, even if they know about and are unsettled by the lawlessness of ICE and CBP, think that harsh enforcement and infringements on immigrant rights don't really affect them personally. They believe they are protected by the firewall of citizenship, sheltered from any harms that may be done to noncitizens. Some may even welcome the idea of roughing up immigrants, who they have been told are lawbreakers. But a rising tide of evidence suggests that Americans' trust in their own government, faith in the good intentions and effectiveness of enforcement, and belief that the power of citizenship will protect them from abuses of power and mistakes may be dangerously naive.

In fact, by overstepping the bounds of the law, overspending already bloated budgets, and overreaching their mandates, the US immigration enforcement apparatus endangers citizens' safety and their civil liberties. As you'll see in this chapter and the next, ICE and CBP abuse US citizens and actively seek to subvert laws and civil liberties that exist to protect against government overreach. ICE and CBP deport Americans—not just accidentally, but through the use of false claims and forcibly extracted fraudulent confessions. They also incarcerate US citizens, sometimes for many months or even years, in facilities that are widely known to be unsafe. When these agencies are caught, they will fight all the way to the highest courts in the land rather than back down. They ignore not just outside legal challenges but even the government's own internal investigations. Neither CBP nor ICE wants us to know what they are up to. CBP has even gone so far as to monitor, detain, and report on journalists who they fear may expose their unsavory and sometimes illegal practices, a fact that should alarm anyone who cherishes the First Amendment and understands how crucial a free press is to a free people.[17] Student demonstrators have been targeted as well, sometimes leading to their being charged with crimes for protesting CBP.[18] The growth of CBP's and ICE's power, the expansion of their jurisdiction, practices and procedures that regularly skirt law and violate human rights, lax documentation and reporting requirements, the agencies' continued immunity from many of the laws and court rulings that regulate governmental and police activities in every other sphere—all of these threaten our security and our liberty.

Let's look more closely at just a few of the ways in which immigration enforcement agencies, policies, and practices flout our laws and principles.

—·—

ICE AND CBP are each large, poorly understood, and dangerous agencies. Although the name *CBP* refers to the border, its jurisdiction encompasses an enormous swath of the country: a hundred miles into the interior from any point on the border. Two-thirds of the US population is located in this region. Not only is CBP larger than any other federal law-enforcement agency; it dwarfs the others. Its twenty-one thousand Border Patrol agents make it larger by far than the FBI (thirteen thousand agents); ICE and Homeland Security Investigations (HSI; around six thousand agents each); Alcohol, Tobacco, Firearms and Explosives (ATF; four thousand); and the Drug Enforcement Administration (DEA; forty-six hundred). CBP has a total of around sixty thousand employees, ICE around twenty thousand (not counting private contractors). But ICE and CBP agents are not always the well-trained professionals that we would hope and imagine them to be. The situation is so bad that in 2014, CBP's head of internal affairs decided to blow the whistle, saying that post-9/11 hiring surges had led to the recruitment of thousands of officers "potentially unfit to carry a badge and gun."[19]

Even after this attempt to spur CBP to clean house, officers have been arrested for drug smuggling, assaults, and an array of other illegal activity. CBP officers are five times more likely than any other law-enforcement agents to be arrested.[20] Every month, it seems, another scandal arises from CBP's corrupt traditions and practices. As we'll see later, lax hiring standards are part of a long-standing institutional culture at CBP that dates to the agency's earliest origins. In one grisly story from 2018, the country learned that a serial killer was working as a CBP agent.[21] From 2005 to 2012, CBP agents were arrested over twenty-one hundred times for crimes.[22] From 2010 to 2015, its agents caused thirty-five casualties in the field.[23] CBP officers have killed people in predictable places like California, Arizona, and Texas but also in Michigan, Washington, and Maine. Ten of the people they killed were US citizens. Six of the others, including three minors, were not even on US soil when they were shot; they were on Mexican soil.[24] At least nine of the thirty-five killed in this period were only throwing rocks when CBP agents shot with intent to kill.[25] Between January 2009 and January 2012, CBP received 809 complaints about its agents' use of excessive force and physical violence.[26] In the next three years, the number of such complaints nearly tripled, to twenty-one hundred.[27] And these are just the reported incidents. We know with certainty that fear keeps a sizable number of people from ever reporting physical and sexual assaults by law-enforcement officers, particularly when someone is afraid that their immigration status or the status of a loved one may make them vulnerable. Yet, from 2005 to 2014, no incidents in which Border Patrol killed people resulted in discipline for the officer, including cases in which video evidence contradicted officers' accounts of what led to the shooting.[28]

CBP officers have abused, assaulted, and sexually molested both children and adults in their custody.[29] The problem goes all the way to the top of the agency: in 2014 a Border Patrol agent raped three women and CBP's commissioner did not even issue a statement until an appeal was made to the secretary of Homeland Security at the time, Jeh Johnson. The commissioner actually cited the plethora of problems with CBP as part of the reason he could not act; his own CBP staff resisted, knowing that investigations would reveal dozens of cases in which agents had transgressed.[30] The ACLU has sued on behalf of a US citizen who was subjected to a strip search, multiple genital and cavity searches, a forced bowel movement, an X-ray, and a CT scan following a false alert by a CBP service canine.[31] Other recountings of similar searches indicate that such incidents probably form part of a pattern of abuse in an agency with a toxic culture and inadequate accountability. In August 2018, an officer was indicted after allegedly strangling

an individual at the San Ysidro port of entry.[32] Accounts of
starvation and sexual assault that happen under CBP care are
particularly hair-raising. After a widely publicized December
2018 incident in which a seven-year-old girl in CBP custody
was denied medical care and subsequently died, DHS issued a
statement blaming the girl's parents for coming to the United
States to ask for asylum.[33] The girl suffered seizures for eight
hours before she died. On the evening I turned this book man-
uscript in to the publisher, I got a news alert informing me
that yet another child—an unaccompanied minor—had died
in CBP custody.[34]

Since CBP is not obligated to record or document any in-
teraction that does not lead to an arrest, we often don't know
exactly what they are doing and to whom they are doing it. In
addition to incidents of violence and fatal neglect, there are
also reports that CBP regularly fails to return property to, or
steals property from,[35] people it is responsible for deporting—
generally, those subject to some form of expedited removal.
CBP agents frequently target areas and people they think are
likely to possess small amounts of marijuana in order to reach
arrest quotas that have been set for them. This practice is unconstitutional but nonetheless persists.

When CBP reaches the limit of what it can accomplish on
its own, it sometimes surreptitiously collaborates with paramilitary organizations and citizen militias organized by self-
appointed civilian border patrols. CBP is not supposed to work
with these groups or their members, but ample documentation
from the groups themselves and from investigative journalists

shows that CBP both chooses to overlook these illegal patrols and collaborates with them by taking information from their members.[36]

It is completely illegal for citizen militia groups to detain anyone, but their members, heavily armed and dressed up to appear as though they are members of a military unit, often do so. Recently it was alleged that one border-patrolling militia, United Constitutional Patriots, held at gunpoint two hundred immigrants, including small children.[37] The most famous of the border-patrolling militias in recent decades is probably the so-called Minutemen. But, as Kathleen Belew chronicles, modern civilian border patrols originated with the KKK. In 1978 the Klan's Operation Hemline was born in a hysteria over the entry of Vietnamese refugees and more general concerns that people seeking refuge were flooding the country—anxieties that remain familiar to us today.[38]

This collaboration with ideologically driven paramilitary organizations is not an aberration for CBP. US border patrol agencies have a long history of working with citizen groups who take the law into their own hands. Civilian groups focused on immigrants have been responsible for mass lynchings, brutal violence, rape, and an array of tactics ranging from ethnic cleansing to daily intimidation. Many of their organizations are founded in direct opposition to the legitimate authority of the US government; they are at their core antigovernment, and some even seek to undermine and eviscerate the government.[39] Many also share a white or Aryan-power ideology that actively seeks race war and ethnic cleansing. In the 1980s, the group

Civilian Military Assistance organized vigilante patrols of the US-Mexico border in sympathy with the white power movement before being funded by the CIA to overthrow the leftist government of Nicaragua.[40]

Whether they claim to or not, militias that take it upon themselves to "police" the border do not know or respect distinctions between citizen and noncitizen, guilty and innocent, legal and illegal. That they are allowed to persist is frightening and has forced some towns to organize independent attempts to repel the advance of militias entering their jurisdictions.[41] An agency of the federal government that has sided and collaborated with militias is an agency that is out of control. Trustworthy government agencies dismantle militias engaged in illegal activities. They certainly shouldn't collaborate with them. CBP has denied collaborating with militias, but the evidence makes clear that it does.[42]

CBP tries to obfuscate and hide its problematic conduct in various other ways as well. It has changed the definition of *complaints* to reduce the number of excessive-force complaints recorded as such.[43] It also makes a distinction between misconduct by its personnel that is classified as "mission compromising" and "non mission compromising." Drug smuggling, for example, is "mission compromising," but sexually assaulting or murdering detainees is "non mission compromising" and is subject to less stringent internal reporting requirements.[44] In other cases, CBP doesn't even bother covering its tracks. Every year since 2010, CBP's own data report that the number of nondeportable people it takes into custody vastly outstrips the number of deportable people it holds. Despite this fact, CBP holds thousands in conditions many liken to concentration camps. At more than one facility, inmates are thrown into a chilled holding room known as the "icebox," in some cases while they are still wet from crossing the Rio Grande. While being held, they are denied regular access to bathrooms; many soil themselves. Food rations might be as meager as two bologna sandwiches shared between a mother and a child over the course of four days.[45] Caging inmates—even children—is a regular occurrence. Government inspectors have found a facility in Texas with a maximum capacity of 125 holding nearly 900 immigrants.[46] Without room to even lie down on the floor, nutrition, sanitation, or other basic necessities, it is no surprise that people die in custody.

ICE appears to be following in the footsteps of CBP, growing more dangerous and emboldened every year in ways that threaten the lives of people in the interior of the country, nowhere near the border. Every year immigration agents hunt down and arrest thousands of people, incarcerating some for months or even years. The number of people in immigration prisons and the steep ascent of those numbers are quite dramatic. In 1994, only around 81,000 people were detained during the entire year. By 2001, before the INS had been absorbed into DHS, it was detaining just over 200,000 people a year.[47] Eleven years later, that number had skyrocketed to almost 464,000.[48] Put another way, in 1994, on any given day, the United States held approximately 6,800 immigrants in detention.[49] In 2019, projections show that we will have 47,000 immigrants incarcerated on any given day.[50] Right now, there are 14,000 children in federal custody, some under the age of five.[51] These are hardly people who need to be incarcerated, particularly young, unaccompanied minors.

Not all the people being detained by ICE are even immigrants; some are US citizens. In 2019 the ACLU issued a report showing that in all likelihood, dozens of US citizens in a Miami detention facility had been detained by ICE with the intent to deport them.[52] The report notes that of 420 "detainer requests" (requests by ICE that someone who is in jail be held after they are set to be released, because ICE believes they are deportable), 83 of those cases were later dismissed, almost certainly because the detainees were US citizens. The ACLU believes that even more of those detained probably were US citizens. The Cato Institute conducted a similar investigation in Texas, finding that in one county (Travis), between 2005 and 2017, ICE targeted at least 228 US citizens for detention deportation.[53] At that rate, Cato extrapolates (using a conservative read of the data) that in the same time period, approximately 3,506 US citizens were targeted for detention and deportation. Similarly, the ACLU suspects that what they uncovered at one facility in Florida means that there are hundreds of cases in that state alone.[54] A research clinic at Northwestern University used Freedom of Information Act (FOIA) requests to uncover hundreds of cases in which US citizens have been detained by ICE. Some of the cases are pending deportation, and, as we will see in the next chapter, some have already resulted in deportation.[55] The researchers for this study had to rely heavily on FOIA requests because ICE did not want to admit to their careless approach to the rights of citizens and noncitizens. According to the Northwestern study, the average length of time that a *US citizen* is held after being picked up by ICE is six months.[56] CBP has also been found detaining children who are US citizens, very likely as a ruse to entrap parents who they suspect are not legal residents.[57]

Whereas anyone who ICE believes is deportable can be detained, Congress has enacted legislation that *requires* the detention of some people who are set to be deported, though it is not always clear that these rules serve a purpose. Since 1996, many immigrants have been detained mandatorily while they await hearings, even when they pose no threat to anyone. Many of those who are detained linger in ICE prisons for months—ten months on average—as they await hearings, deportation, or release. Of those, half will appeal their decision, forcing them to remain in prison for almost a full year, on average.[58] If a judge does say they qualify for bail, the amount can range from $1,500 to over $80,000.[59]

The array of circumstances under which people are being imprisoned is expanding. For example, some people in ICE custody have entered the country without an inspection because they want to claim asylum. This is legal, as is indicating at a border crossing that one wants to claim asylum. ICE does not *have* to incarcerate these people. ICE can parole anyone in its custody who indicates that they wish to claim asylum, if that individual passes the "credible fear" interview, the process that determines whether they are fleeing their home country for a reason that would entitle them to asylum. (People who do not pass their credible fear interview can request review of their case by a judge if they know they have this right. Barring that request, or upon a judge's affirmation of the initial decision, failing the interview is followed by removal from the country.) Parole allows them to be out of prison while they wait for their case to receive a hearing. This is generally a safe practice. Asylum seekers who show a credible fear of persecution in their home country almost always come back for their hearings; their rates of attendance in recent years have been around 96 percent.[60] When they are offered the chance to participate in family-case-management pilot programs, which have been discontinued by the Trump administration, the rate at which they return for their hearings is 100 percent.[61] (Costs per day for such programs are a fraction of the costs of incarceration.) Simply making it possible for people to get to their hearings would likely be enough to guarantee an extremely high rate of attendance. In 2012, around 80 percent of all people who passed their credible fear interview were paroled. As recently as 2015, 50 percent were paroled while awaiting their hearing. Anecdotal evidence suggests that since 2017, the rate has sunk as low as 10 percent.[62] These are people who pose no threat to anyone and who have experienced a documented trauma. Why are we keeping asylum seekers in prison, causing them immense distress and costing taxpayers huge sums?

The US government has gone to great lengths to hide and even lie about how long it is keeping some immigrants in prison. A brief to the Supreme Court challenging a 2001 ruling showed that the federal government had misrepresented statistics that the court explicitly relied on when rejecting a constitutional challenge to the detention regime. The government had previously told the Supreme Court that immigrants who appealed their deportation were detained an average of about five months, but admitted fifteen years later that it had significantly understated average detention durations, and that in fact its own data showed at the time that the average length of detention for this group was more than a year (382 days).[63] Generally speaking, and somewhat counterintuitively, the immigrants most likely to win their cases (detainees who were able to afford legal representation and find a reputable lawyer) were imprisoned for the longest periods of time. For represented detainees subject to mandatory detention, average case duration was still around ten months.[64]

Conditions in ICE facilities are often subhuman. Between 2010 and 2016, ICE officials indicated to investigative journalists that they received thirty-three thousand complaints of physical and sexual abuse occurring in their facilities.[65] This may be an undercount if, as is likely, many people do not report instances of sexual assault and violence. Sexual violence appears to account for the largest proportion of the complaints. ICE didn't even record sexual assault complaint data until 2014.[66] *The Intercept* documented a horrific instance in which an employee of a private detention facility maced an inmate, filmed her showering, and then sat on her as though he were riding a horse, "his erect penis on her butt."[67] But even when inmates are not being assaulted, they are abused in other ways.

The Intercept published an account of a contractor-run facility in which inmates who attempted suicide were described as "suicide failures."[68] Volunteer lawyers regularly report dreadful practices and circumstances.

Twenty-two adults died in ICE custody between 2017 and 2019.[69] In some cases, internal documents have shown that the US government believes that the deaths were preventable, and in a grim nod to this fact, ICE stopped updating its website acknowledging "deaths in custody" in 2017.[70] DHS's own inspector general has found that ICE's private contractors are not held accountable for abuses that are discovered; often their response has been to try to exempt the facilities and contractors from requirements meant to protect inmates.[71] Despite these abuses, ICE has recently flouted restrictions placed on it by Congress, contracting with a number of privately run facilities in the Deep South, some of which are known to be operated in dangerous ways.[72]

Young people ensnared by ICE and CBP are particularly vulnerable.[73] Thousands of allegations of sexual abuse have surfaced following the family-separation crisis that began in 2018.[74] But the problems neither begin nor end with that crisis. For example, immigrant teens at the Shenandoah Valley Juvenile Center (a facility run by several Virginia counties and cities that has received $31.4 million in federal funding since 2009) have reported repeated mistreatment and abuse.[75] Teenagers have been strapped to a metal chair, sometimes after being stripped nearly naked. They have been restrained by their feet, arms, and waist, sometimes for days at a time. If guards believe that a prisoner will react, for example by spitting on them, they might cloak the detainee in a hood that covers his or her entire face. Parties to a lawsuit against the Shenandoah center reported that being tied to the chair was a common punishment.[76] An eighteen-year-old Guatemalan teenager who was caught by immigration officers after running away from home said that they did not allow him or others detained at the center to take bathroom breaks, so they urinated on themselves while they were strapped in the chair. Other reports about a Texas center detail guards punishing inmates with beatings, long periods in solitary confinement, and forced treatment with psychotropics.[77] Whistleblowers reporting on ICE abuses before and after Trump came to office drew special attention to the deadly circumstances children face in family detention, pointing to the frequency with which children's fingers were crushed in doors meant to be handled by adults, and even more chilling instances in which an infant's brain-bleed went undiagnosed.[78]

ICE has been repeatedly accused of abusing pregnant women in its custody. In July 2018, BuzzFeed documented that pregnant women in detention were being abused and were denied proper medical care.[79] DHS's own records show that twenty-eight pregnant women miscarried while in DHS custody between January 2017 and March 2019.[80] In one case, ICE agents are alleged to have taken a group of suspected undocumented workers detained in a Nebraska raid, including two pregnant women, on a two-hour drive in hundred-degree heat with no climate control or water. When the detainees asked for cool air, the agents turned on the heater instead.

Equally chilling is what we are learning about plans to militarize immigration enforcement. Federal records indicate that ICE's enforcement and removal officers are being trained to use stun grenades, flash bangs, chemical agents, and M4 assault rifles. ICE is also building an "urban warfare" training facility. The militarization of immigration enforcement is a relatively new phenomenon, but all indications are that its scope is expanding. It currently encompasses an array of weapons. The M4 is typically used by the armed forces; it is the primary service weapon for the Marine Corps. ICE and CBP now have approximately thirteen thousand M4 rifles between them. ICE has signed a $15 million contract with Colt's Manufacturing Company to maintain these weapons. Existing records show that the agency claims a current "annual need" for training up to 160 agents quarterly, for a total of 640 each year.

Arming immigration agents with military-grade weapons will change these agencies. Even if they were all "good guys with guns" (which they're clearly not), research on policing shows that when civilian police forces are militarized, fatalities increase and the organizations fundamentally change the way they perceive and execute their missions.[81] Militarized law enforcement is prone to dehumanizing its targets, denying their rights, and ignoring consequential legal distinctions, including those among classes of noncitizens such as asylum seekers, undocumented workers, and legal immigrants.[82]

We're not a society in which having armed soldiers in our daily lives and enforcing our laws is standard practice, so giving immigration enforcement agents military-grade weapons is exceptionally alarming. Also alarming are the multiple studies showing that many of the agents working for these organizations are not well vetted.[83] And even when they are well vetted, the larger systemic risks of militarization remain. Thirteen thousand M4 rifles can easily become fifty thousand in a few short years, once a precedent has been set.

Even supposing there were no risks to militarizing immigration enforcement, it is unclear what threats exist that could reasonably justify the "annual need" for military-grade weapons claimed by ICE and CBP. In fact, there appears to be almost no threat that would generate any need for CBP and ICE to militarize. I say "appears" because the records of the attacks they supposedly need this kind of weaponry for are poorly kept. The data are spotty because no procedures are in place for the formal reporting of incidents in which firearms would be required for either self-protection or purposes of law enforcement—a lack of standards the Office of the Inspector General (OIG) has criticized.[84] Instead, CBP and ICE agents self-report, via informal means, the number of assaults targeting them. And CBP counts assaults in absurd ways. For example, one incident in which six perpetrators threw three types of objects (rocks, bottles, tree branches) at seven agents during a brief encounter was counted as 126 separate assaults.[85] Even so, the number of attacks on ICE and CBP officers is low. Between 2014 and 2017, there were a whopping seven convictions for attacks on ICE officers.[86] The number of attacks on CBP is higher, but ultimately those numbers are insubstantial as well. Between 2010 and 2017, CBP officers reported having been injured 195 times by assaults.[87] It is hard to understand how this justifies the acquisition of military-grade weapons, especially given the risks that militarization incurs. In fact, almost all fatalities associated with working for CBP are the result of accidents like falls and drowning. Between 2003 and 2017, only three of the thirty-three reported CBP agent fatalities could be traced to "hostiles" who harmed an agent on the job.[88]

The immigration enforcement accountability crisis reaches the highest levels of the US government. The 2018 family-separation crisis was spawned by the Department of Justice's Zero Tolerance program, which explicitly denied forms of relief that had once been available to undocumented parents entering the United States with children. The policy forced the separation of parents and children, some of whom were ultimately lost and could not be returned to their parents. The ACLU sued, and federal courts gave DHS until July 26, 2018, to reunite children with parents from whom they had been separated at the border. But DHS did not comply, in some cases because they had not taken enough care with their record keeping to be able to comply, and months later hundreds of children remained separated from their families. Arguments were made that some children whom the Office of Refugee Resettlement had placed with sponsor families during their separation should not be reunited with their actual families because doing so would cause trauma.[89] What recourse anyone has is unclear. As one commentator put it, "The courts do not have a standing army."[90] There is no one to enforce the deadline, just as no one prevented almost five hundred parents from being deported before their children could be found. The Department of Justice, which had initiated Zero Tolerance, naturally did not push back against the implementation and consequences of its own policy. Even after the courts had declared the policy illegal, Donald Trump was so intent on reviving it that many believe he forced out former DHS secretary Kirstjen Nielsen for refusing to reinstate it. Shortly after he did so, the public learned that there were likely many more lost children than was initially reported.[91] By April 2019, the government was acknowledging that at least 1,475 of the 7,000 children that had been separated from their parents were lost and could not be accounted for.[92] DHS admitted that reuniting the remaining children with their parents was probably impossible.

CBP has also been roundly criticized for its practices by both internal DHS inspectors and outsiders who follow the agency. The DHS Office of the Inspector General—in a report that featured a recommendation that CBP explore nonlethal alternatives for addressing rock-throwing, a finding CBP had redacted from the public release of the study—found that CBP officers do not understand their own agency's use-of-force policies. A recent Government Accountability Office (GAO) report on CBP reporting of employee misconduct shows that CBP refuses to report most cases to the Joint Intake Center, which is meant to monitor and investigate misconduct issues.[93] The Police Executive Research Forum writes that CBP is "not as diligent with follow up investigation and evaluations of cases where shots were fired and injuries were not confirmed," as compared with cases where confirmation *is* made, leaving open the possibility that in cases with unconfirmed outcomes, more injuries and fatalities occur than are officially reported.[94]

It is troubling enough that a very large, lawless arm of the US government fails to respect the rights of either citizens or noncitizens. But it is even more disturbing when those same federal agencies ignore internal investigations or go to court to fight for the power to deny people their rights, and upon losing in court do not—and cannot—comply with court orders under federal law. Why are ICE, CBP, and DHS more invested in defending themselves in court than they are in figuring out why their employees and their policies are doing things to land them in court in the first place? And to whom, if anyone, are our government agencies accountable, if not the courts and government investigators? If government agencies can operate without accountability to the law, what are the implications for a democratic political system?

Much of the time in a democratic society we do not and cannot rely on the threat of punishment to motivate civil servants and law-enforcement officers. It is simply too difficult and expensive to constantly police all levels of the government. Instead, we rely on the fact that those who lead and staff our governmental institutions will respect the law precisely because they work for the government, in a public service capacity. When we've reached the point where that no longer happens, the corruption of those institutions becomes a threat to the rule of law in ways that reverberate throughout a democracy, slowly and permanently cracking its foundations. If the very agencies responsible for law enforcement are also the institutions that cannot be trusted or held accountable for their actions, everyone's rights have been compromised. As we will see, when law-enforcement agencies actively seek to push or overstep the boundaries of their work and the law, when they are rewarded for being sadistic and escape punishment for breaking the law, they stop caring about other constraints, including those that are supposed to protect citizens from being targeted by immigration officials. And the more they get away with, the more emboldened they will become.

—•—

AMERICANS MAY NOT know how dangerous or expensive the government's immigration apparatus is, but they do know that they are not strongly in favor of mass deportation and that they in general support immigration. Two-thirds of all Americans say they are not in favor of trying to deport all undocumented immigrants.[95] Opinion polls suggest that, even after decades of sustained nativist activism, most Americans find images of abuse profoundly troubling and agree that immigrants and asylum seekers should be welcomed. Support of immigrants is strong even in states where residents see the most undocumented immigration and government enforcement intrusion.[96]

Yet in spite of public support for immigration, evidence that undocumented immigration is declining, and the repeated grave misconduct of ICE and CBP agents, taxpayers fund astronomical budgets for immigration enforcement that often outpace the already generous congressional budget appropriations the agencies receive annually. ICE generally overspends its budget as a means to push for future increases in its budget, which it then overspends. To do this, ICE drains money from other federal agencies, including the Federal Emergency Management Agency (FEMA).[97] ICE also draws manpower from USCIS, exacerbating existing visa and citizenship-processing backlogs.[98] In 2019, the Pentagon diverted $1 billion of US Army money for DHS activity related to the border wall.[99] And ICE siphons away resources of local law enforcement through agreements that engage police in immigration enforcement activities that ought to be the responsibility of the federal government.

The push to incarcerate as many people as possible, regardless of whether they pose any threat to anyone, is a big part of the problem. Each adult detention bed costs $126.46 per day on average. An immigration expert and reporter for the *Los Angeles Times* estimates conservatively that the United States spends $5 million each day on detention.[100] Other experts think this number is actually too low.[101] Detaining immigrant children is now at least a $1 billon industry—a tenfold increase over the past decade, according to an Associated Press analysis.[102] A family-detention bed costs $161.36 per day on average. Detaining children alone in places like the tent city in Tornillo, Texas, can cost over $700 per day per child.[103] The US government has slowly been moving away from alternatives to detention that are more cost-effective and humane, such as community-based release and discharging unaccompanied children into the care of family members. Health and Human Services (HHS) grants for foster care, child welfare, and shelters for detained unaccompanied and separated children went from $74.5 million in 2007 to $958 million in 2017—a staggering 1185.90 percent increase. In 2018, HHS issued requests for bids for five projects that could represent more than $500 million in spending for beds, foster and therapeutic care, and "secure care," where they will employ guards for their facilities. An HHS spokesman said the agency will award bids based on how many minors they admit into the program. In the past ten years, the recipients that have been awarded the most money from such grants have been Southwest Key ($1.39 billion) and Baptist Child and Family Services ($942 million). Southwest Key took custody of hundreds of migrant children during the 2018 family-separation crisis in which very young children were taken from their parents. Since that time, however, Southwest Key was exposed by a *New York Times* investigation for using government grant money in unethical ways that enriched the organization's founder, Juan Sanchez, and his friends.[104] The *Washington Post* reports that in 2017, Sanchez earned $3.6 million in total compensation.[105]

The costs of our out-of-control immigration regime will skyrocket even further if an immigration reform deal is struck that accedes to demands for a border wall. The GAO has estimated that it could cost $6.5 million per mile to build a single-layer fence, plus $4.2 million per mile for roads and more fencing.[106] Even very conservative estimates of total construction costs for the fence approach $20 billion.[107] Those estimates do not include the costs of maintaining the fence, patrolling parts of the border where the terrain cannot be walled, and surveilling or staffing the fence for the inevitable attempts to pass over and under it.

Whether or not exorbitant expenditures for a pointless border wall are ever approved, taxpayers are already spending plenty for the Department of Homeland Security not to prioritize the job it was created to do. As we dig more deeply into the story of how this country's taxpayers ended up paying so much for the privilege of ceding our core rights to immigration control agencies, we'll see that the Department of Homeland Security was sold to Americans after 9/11 as a way to protect against another terrorist attack. In fact, starting in 2017, the Trump administration dismantled and cut multiple programs that were created in response to the terrorist attacks of 9/11 without even a serious review.[108]

Homeland Security Investigations (HSI), the branch of ICE responsible for counterterrorism work, is an anemic part of the agency. HSI is supposed to work with federal, state, local, and international partners to identify and dismantle transnational criminal organizations and address other criminal activities pertaining to national security and global security. It is the organization most directly responsible for preventing security threats and terrorist attacks in and on the United States. And security threats to Americans do exist; they just aren't related to immigration or immigrants. The threat of foreign-born persons in the United States without authorization committing terrorism is small, and it is downright infinitesimal in comparison with other threats, including domestic terrorism. So minuscule is the threat of immigrant terrorism that DHS has openly lied to inflate its operations in that regard.[109] So has one of the most prominent anti-immigration organizations in the country, Center for Immigration Studies (CIS); an investigation of its own fact sheet on terrorists crossing the US border with Mexico shows that of the fifteen people apprehended at or near the southern border between 2003 and 2018 on suspicions of having a connection to terror or terrorism, exactly none could be shown to have been planning to commit acts of terror on US soil.[110] This may explain the fact that the budget and staff resources allocated to HSI are dwarfed by those accorded to the branches charged with performing immigration functions unrelated to terrorism. HSI's position within DHS is so bad that in 2018, nineteen agents who worked for HSI sent a letter to DHS secretary Kirstjen Nielsen asking her to split HSI from the agency, and more specifically to separate HSI from any association with enforcement agencies like CBP and ICE.[111] These agents expressed the widely held view that ICE and CBP are now so openly abusive and corrupt that any association with them thwarts HSI's mission. The agents further claimed that they are too poorly funded to successfully execute their actual mission. However, the fact that this underresourcing and lack of autonomy from ICE has not led to a foreign-born person executing a terrorist attack in the United States since HSI was created suggests that HSI is *not* underfunded or constrained. Its real purpose, scaring Americans into paying for an immigration enforcement apparatus that serves mostly bad ends, doesn't require big budgets or autonomy from ICE. But even as the undocumented-immigrant population has shrunk and then stabilized, our enforcement arms race has only ramped up.

—.—

EVERY SOCIETY IMPOSES boundaries and exclusions. But beware the society that starts to redraw its lines, tightening the drawstrings on its democracy and emboldening its most abusive institutions. Access to rights may recede further and further, until few people can claim protection by the law of the land. Along the way, the boundaries between citizen and noncitizen will be revealed to be quite fragile. Agencies and policies that gradually eat away at core rights eventually push law and order out of reach for all of us. For their roles in these processes, already well underway, ICE, CBP, and DHS, more than any immigrant, pose a grave threat to law and order in our society.

Once the last domino falls, no one is safe. Robert Michels, one of the twentieth century's most influential sociologists, explained the reason that the dominoes are likely to fall in one of social science's most famous and undisputed axioms: the Iron Law of Oligarchy. The theory proposes that bureaucracies and agencies, left unchecked, will always grow and spread, expanding the scope of their power and budgets and suffocating individual rights along the way. It is a law of oligarchy because the result is the erosion of democracy and its replacement with forms of government that concentrate power in the hands of a very few people who control the agencies and organizations. That is why bureaucracies and bureaucrats require supervision and checks on their power. But right now, immigration enforcement is not subject to the same checks as other law enforcement in the United States. In the next chapter, we're going to zero in on a few specific ways that ICE and CBP are being allowed to operate outside the boundaries of both the Constitution and ordinary legal practice. Then we'll step back and look at how this country created such a disastrous immigration enforcement regime and what we can do about it.

CHAPTER TWO

Constitutionally Unshackled

I HAVE DESCRIBED THE CULTURE OF IMPUNITY THAT PERVADES IMMI-gration enforcement in the United States. Impunity—the idea that illegal and patently immoral behavior goes unpunished— is hard to fathom for those of us who have always had faith in the rule of law and all the benefits that come with trustworthy institutions. We may be uncomfortable adjusting to the idea that our laws, the people who enforce those laws, and even our courts are corrupt. But overwhelming evidence shows that we cannot trust our immigration enforcement agencies to respect our rights or our laws. We may not yet understand how we are affected, and we may think we are invulnerable—protected by race, citizenship, or names that sound "American." But those distinctions don't matter as much to ICE and CBP as one might hope, and the longer their power goes unchecked the more of us will be caught up in their machinations. Ultimately, no citizen escapes unscathed when the rule of law on which democracies are founded is eroded.

Multiple sources feed the culture of impunity that infects immigration enforcement. Later I will review some of the history behind lawless immigration enforcement in this country. But one of the most enduring reasons immigration enforcement agents and agencies assume they can get away with operating outside the bounds of the law is that they start out exempt from a few critical legal and constitutional constraints that apply to other types of law enforcement. These exceptions contribute to a sense that they do not have to play by the same rules others do or honor our rights.

For CBP, an important source of the agency's sense of exceptionalism can be traced to the absence of constitutional restrictions that apply to other law-enforcement groups. In the case of ICE, Congress has legislated away the obligation for ICE to provide many of its targets even a semblance of due process. In both cases, what at first seem to be innocuous or confined exceptions to the ordinary constraints on law-enforcement behavior actually allow the boundaries of the law and the Constitution to be stretched and abused, carving out huge powers for the immigration enforcement apparatus in the United States. The result, consequential not only for immigrants but for all Americans, has been an erosion of the most fundamental rights and protections on which a constitutional democracy rests.

———•——

MOST OF THE US population—about two-thirds—lives in the official CBP border zone that stretches around the entire physical boundary of the country, land and sea, and reaches into the interior one hundred miles at every point. The reach of this exceptional zone was originally an area in which district directors of the earliest Border Patrol were taking liberties that at best stretched the Constitution and at worst directly violated it. Congress later blessed the Border Patrol's expanded understanding of its own powers as exercised in what Congress called a "reasonable distance" from the border.[1] Congress's move was validated in a 1957 decision by the US attorney general to define the border zone as occupying territory a "reasonable distance" from the external boundary of the United States and set its limits at "100 air miles from any external boundary of the United States."[2] At the time, there were only eleven hundred Border Patrol officers, and the technology at their disposal was rudimentary. In 2019, there are twenty-one thousand agents, some heavily armed, operating in this exceptional zone.

Within the official border zone, CBP can exploit exemptions from parts of normal US constitutional constraints with which the police, FBI, or any other law-enforcement agencies must comply. These restrictions affect how CBP handles vehicle stops, searches, questioning, and even entry onto people's property.

CBP's exceptional status encompasses several facets. The first has to do with how CBP can justify its searches in the first place. According to the Supreme Court, all vehicle stops constitute a "seizure" for the purposes of the Fourth Amendment, whose stated purpose is to protect us from unreasonable searches and seizures.[3] These stops and their consequences can be harrowing, not only for undocumented persons but for their families, and also for the many citizens and legal residents who endure them. CBP checks have particularly high stakes, and CBP has a great deal of latitude in pursuing their checks. But the federal regulations issued in 1957 created a uniquely expansive definition of a "reasonable" search for CBP, freeing them from important restrictions imposed by the Fourth Amendment. For all other officers of the law, reasonable search must be preceded by what is known as probable cause as well as a warrant. These are required before agents can engage in a search or can seize property. But the 1957 regulations for CBP effectively remove these constraints on CBP searches and seizures in a twenty-five-mile zone from the border to the interior. In that zone, CBP is allowed to search and seize people's property for less than "probable cause" and with no warrant. This allows them to "board and search for aliens any vessel within the territorial waters of the United States and any railway car, aircraft, conveyance, or vehicle, and within a reasonable distance of twenty-five miles from any such external boundary to have access to private lands, but not dwellings, for the purpose of patrolling the border to prevent the illegal entry of aliens into the United States."[4]

CBP can enter people's vehicles and go onto people's land (but not into their homes) without first getting a warrant to do so.

In a 1976 Supreme Court decision, *Martinez-Fuerte,* the court extended CBP's power in the entire hundred-mile border zone, affirming the constitutionality of almost any checkpoint in that zone whose primary purpose is immigration enforcement. CBP checkpoints can be fixed or roving. At fixed checkpoints operated by CBP, agents can also engage in searches without the requirement that they have suspicion and without a warrant. A roving checkpoint is wherever in the hundred-mile zone CBP decides to go, although we'll see that they violate even this boundary.

At fixed checkpoints, the Supreme Court has decided that routine, suspicionless, warrantless searches, seizures,[5] and limited questioning[6] are reasonable even *without* what it calls "individualized suspicion." *Individualized suspicion* is the legal system's phrase to refer to treating any potential suspect as an individual rather than extrapolating from past cases, as someone using racial profiling might do. The requirement that law-enforcement agents demonstrate that they are applying a standard of individualized suspicion is what protects us from being profiled (by race or other variables) and forbids law-enforcement officers from arbitrarily targeting people or harassing them. Except, of course, CBP agents. In plain language this means that CBP can engage in acts that, for other law-enforcement officers, would be considered profiling.

In 1975, the Supreme Court finally established limits on when CBP patrols can stop and search motorists within the United States.[7] Unfortunately, the court gave Border Patrol such wide latitude that it practically invited the agency to engage in profiling. The 1975 case, called *Brignoni-Ponce*, gave Border Patrol officers permission to stop someone as long as they could make a "rational inference" from an "articulable fact" about that person to support their suspicion that the vehicle contained someone undocumented. The court gave a list of examples of what sort of "fact" it thought would support the inference of unlawful presence, which is full of surprising and often irrelevant characteristics. Of particular note is that the court blessed making a judgment based on someone's appearance or even the appearance of their car. For example, if someone has the "characteristic appearance of persons who live in Mexico,"[8] such as "the mode of dress and haircut" of a Mexican person, that was enough. The highest court in the land thereby equated *looking foreign* (according to the opinion of a CBP officer) with *individualized suspicion*. In doing so, the court ensured that CBP could get away with abusive behavior like harassing and arresting US citizens for doing totally legal and innocuous things, like speaking Spanish.[9]

These are significant incursions on the Fourth Amendment rights of US citizens. Even if CBP used its extraconstitutional powers in only the precise ways they are intended to be used, they would be highly consequential for citizens and noncitizens alike. But CBP doesn't always use its powers responsibly.

CBP claims it uses its power to conduct searches and seizures in ways that would be illegal for other law-enforcement agencies because it must do so in order to effectively deter unauthorized immigration. Their deterrent mandate was the original justification for putting CBP under the authority of DHS back in 2003. Yet evidence suggests that CBP uses its authority not just to deter people attempting to enter the country without permission but also to bully long-term residents and citizens indiscriminately. Here's an excerpt from an NYU Law School immigration clinic report on CBP bus and train stops in New York:

> In Rochester, New York, between the years 2006–2009, 76% of those arrested during CBP bus and train raids had been living in the United States for longer than one year, and 12% of those arrested had been present in the country for more than ten years. Of the 2,743 people arrested during CBP transportation raids in Rochester in that four-year span, only seven were arrested at entry and fifteen were arrested within seventy-two hours of crossing the border.[10]

CBP was given the powers it has at the border to prevent unauthorized entry, but most people that CBP arrests at checkpoints are not deportable. If the idea is for CBP to guard the border and deter or detain people trying to cross without authorization, well, this is not what they are doing. Instead, they are harassing longtime residents and putting out indiscriminate dragnets that ensnare all of us. And they're not even doing that very efficiently. For example, according to an ACLU class action filed in January 2014,[11] two-thirds of the checkpoint encounters listed in the complaint included false alerts. As a scholar at the Cato Institute said, "There is a mentality operating that says that these checkpoints are essential to countering illegal immigration and all the data says the opposite. . . . They're completely ineffectual at actually stopping illegal immigration."[12] Observe how little each agent accomplishes (recall that the number of agents has increased from eleven hundred in the late 1950s to twenty-one thousand today):

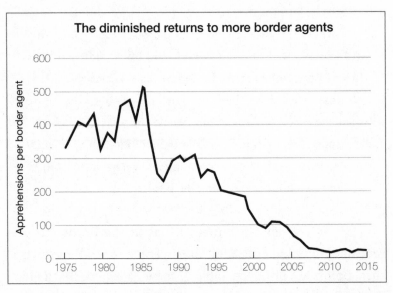

The diminished returns to more border agents. *Source:* US Customs and Border Protection, reproduced in Jeremy L. Neufeld, "Law Enforcement at the Border: Staffing, Corruption, and Oversight," policy brief, Niskanen Center, May 16, 2018, https:// niskanencenter.org/wp-content/uploads/2018/05/Law-Enforcement-at-the-Border -Brief.pdf.

And even if the rules by which they are expected to operate were not exceptional interpretations of very clearly articulated constitutional principles, CBP often ignores the hundred-mile and twenty-five-mile distance restrictions on its various activities. In one instance, CBP agents stopped Senator Patrick Leahy 125 miles south of the border. During the stop, when the agent was asked about his authority to perform the search, he pointed to his gun and said, "That's all the authority I need."[13] No one ever accused CBP agents of being exceptionally clever, but even so that moment marks a low point in strategic behavior.

In another case, CBP agents entered a private citizen's land multiple times without a warrant, probable cause, consent, or emergency; installed cameras on the property without the knowledge or permission of the owner; and swarmed the property for reasons not obviously related to immigration enforcement. They also invaded the owner's privacy in numerous other ways.[14] At best, this is questionably legal behavior. For example, in the case of the secret cameras installed on a private citizen's property without his or her knowledge, the property in question was actually *thirty-five miles* from the border—outside the twenty-five-mile zone in which such an action could have even conceivably been legal. This is neither an accident nor a lapse; CBP openly self-describes its statutory authority in ways that flagrantly exceed what the Supreme Court has said the Constitution allows. And often, no one disciplines the CBP, least of all its umbrella agency, DHS. As the next chapter will show, border patrol agencies in the United States have long carried on the practice of breaking laws and asking for those laws to be changed rather than simply doing their job within the confines of the law.

———•——

IT IS BAD enough that CBP is allowed to come onto our land, profile us, and stop us when we travel. But just imagine what it would be like to have the US government show up and, fully within the limits of the law, take your home and your land. For some people who reside near the border, this is already a reality; their land has been seized in order to build border fencing. And as anyone concerned about immigration in the United States knows, one of Donald Trump's recurring campaign promises was to fully enclose the southern border with a wall. Let's take a moment to consider what it means for the government to build a border barrier that runs through your property.

Border wall politics date back to the early 1990s, and ever since passage of the 2005 Real ID Act, DHS has had extremely broad authority to waive "all legal requirements" necessary to ensure expeditious construction of border barriers.[15] Under the law related to eminent domain, the government can claim land it believes it requires for a public purpose, compensating its owners according to its own formulae.

The last major push to extend the barrier started in 2006, with the Secure Fence Act. That bill identified five construction areas totaling 850 miles, later amended to 700 miles. After that construction push, a generous estimate suggests that one-tenth of the US border had been fenced. Just to accomplish that feat required four hundred lawsuits to claim property via eminent domain. Some of those suits are still being litigated.

DHS planned to complete 370 miles of border fence (out of a total of 700 required miles) by December 2008. In that year, the GAO issued a report revealing that 54 percent of the project (200 miles) was to be constructed on private property.[16] Four hundred eighty landowners were contacted about having their property surveyed; 332 agreed and 148 refused. A second letter threatening court action induced half of the 148 to agree to land surveying. At the time, many people's land was seized with the promise of forthcoming compensation. However, when the federal government and the landowner cannot agree on a compensation amount, the landowners can remain uncompensated for years—some as long as a decade—despite the fact that their land has already been taken.[17] Ultimately, four hundred condemnation actions[18] (i.e., eminent domain lawsuits) were filed in 2008 and 2009. As of 2017, there were ninety legal cases still pending from the land the government sought to obtain after the Secure Fence Act in the years 2006–2010.[19]

While no construction has begun under Trump, and it isn't at all clear that construction can begin without congressional approval, after the 2016 election some borderland landowners received a document from the US government called a "Declaration of Takings."[20] In some cases, land that may be taken has been in the owners' hands for many generations.[21] Based on recent experience and what we know about who owns land near the border, we can anticipate that Trump's highly ambitious plans for border wall construction will require many disruptive seizures of private property. DHS estimates that only a third of the remaining land on which Trump proposes to build is owned by the federal government.[22] The rest is privately owned, state owned, or the property of indigenous tribes. Most of the privately owned land is in Texas. The US government would probably have to deal with (and spend taxpayer dollars litigating) thousands of lawsuits if it seized all the property necessary to complete the wall along the Texas border alone. It seems likely that further action—even if sanctioned by Congress—will unleash an unprecedented number of lawsuits against the government. Perhaps even more troubling is the erosion of trust that would result from the degradation of our property rights after such an immense appropriation of private property.

—·—

WHAT I HAVE been describing are violations of property and privacy rights the effects of which run to the very core of our understanding of autonomy and free movement. If we cannot move about without being harassed by government agents with guns, or trust the government not to take our homes and our land, we're losing our grip on the very rights that our founders sought to guarantee when they wrote our Constitution.

But the problem is even more fundamental than that. In any democracy, it should be the case that all persons have a set of special rights that help them defend all their other rights against abuse, particularly by powerful law-enforcement agencies. In the United States we refer to this category of safeguards

as "due process." Due process rights help people protect themselves from being abused, imprisoned indefinitely, or incarcerated for illegitimate reasons. They are the bulwark shielding
each of us from something disastrous like languishing in prison
when we haven't been charged with a crime, or being punished
arbitrarily for a crime we did not commit. Due process also
ensures that we each get a fair chance to prove our innocence if
we are accused of a crime. It is a legal concept that dates back to
the Magna Carta and has been considered fundamental to the
rule of law in the United States since its founding. Due process
is not supposed to be reserved for specific people—for example, citizens—or to apply only in specific circumstances. The
principle derives its importance from the fact that it is intended
to apply to *all* people within the country's borders. But ICE
and CBP have to a shocking degree managed to carve out ever-
expanding spaces where due process is not honored.

Although due process isn't going to protect anyone from
agents that shoot and kill both US citizens and immigrants, it
should at least ensure that people being charged with crimes
or being thrown out of the country receive their day in court.
That is not happening. Given that deportation is at stake for
everyone who is apprehended and detained by ICE, one would
expect that all people detained at least have their cases heard
by an immigration judge. After all, a system of justice built on
the concept of due process should ensure that everyone has a
chance to show that a mistake has been made and they ought
not to be deported. But for people targeted by ICE, how much
due process they receive hinges on how ICE has classified them;

some ICE classifications allow ICE to deport people before they have had even a shred of due process.

Unfortunately, few people who end up deported by ICE or CBP are able to obtain legal representation, which can be quite costly. CBP has invested in trying to ensure that immigrants can't get lawyers by surveilling, harassing, and detaining some of the leaders of organizations that provide pro bono representation.[23] Shockingly, in a Clinton-era program (ramped up during the Obama administration) designed to encourage immigrants to waive their rights, at least one Legal Aid lawyer collaborated with DHS to trick immigrants into signing away their rights by misleadingly telling them they had no avenues for relief.[24] The overall result of these obstacles is that only a small minority of people at risk of being deported—around 15 percent—even appear before a judge.[25] Instead, the vast majority are set for what is called "expedited removal," with no chance to prove that they ought to be allowed to stay, or they are just expelled under different legal circumstances. Many of these deportations happen at the border. In removal proceedings termed "administrative" or "expedited," deportations happen so quickly that they effectively deny people any due process or proper review of their case, let alone a hearing in front of an immigration judge. This has been the case since Congress passed harshly punitive legislation in 1996.

Fewer than half of all noncitizens living in the United States who are apprehended by ICE or CBP see their cases go before a judge at all. So-called administrative removals allow ICE officers to deport any noncitizen convicted of what is known as an "aggravated felony" who is not either a lawful permanent resident or a conditional permanent resident when removal proceedings begin. The class of crimes known as aggravated felonies, which I'll discuss in more detail later, is made up of mostly nonviolent crimes, including many fairly innocuous misdemeanors. But aggravated felonies come with extra consequences, and they form a legal category that exists only for noncitizens. Citizens cannot be charged with an aggravated felony. This legal quirk exists for the express purpose of targeting and deporting both legal and undocumented immigrants. Expedited removals result in deportation for people who recently arrived but lack a legal status that allows them to be formally "admitted," or for any immigrant convicted of an aggravated felony who is not a lawful permanent resident.

When it comes to expedited removal, individual ICE and CBP agents act as both prosecutor and judge, charging someone with being deportable and then issuing the "removal order" that begins their deportation process. In addition, ICE can simply have immigrants' earlier orders of removal reinstated; most people who have been deported once will, if they return, be ordered deported without so much as a hearing (even if they might otherwise qualify for some type of status).[26] Such rules ensure that people are deported quickly, before a judge can hear their case and decide whether they are actually eligible for deportation and whether their deportation serves a purpose.

When people faced with immigration-related charges do qualify for a hearing, they often face daunting and unexpected challenges in their attempts to prove that they should not be deported. Immigration removals are classified as civil rather than criminal because immigration violations are not violations of criminal law. But in civil proceedings such as these there is no right to counsel, so the court does not provide legal services to those who cannot afford or find an attorney. We know with great certainty that having access to a lawyer vastly improves the likelihood of a fair proceeding that accurately reflects the circumstances and evidence of a case.[27] However, because we are in the midst of a long-standing effort to make it easy for the government to deport as many people as possible, anyone caught up in ICE's web has fewer opportunities than ever to hire a lawyer, should they be fortunate enough to be able to afford one and to locate a reliable one. Many people ensnared in immigration proceedings do not receive adequate time even to file documents showing that they should not be deported. Some people are deported when they are in the middle of their own legal proceedings.[28] Their lawyers and families report that once people are taken into ICE custody, they are often moved around before their trial and then denied access to phones, so that it becomes impossible for counsel and loved ones to find them, let alone ensure they are safe and prepare a case.[29] Although recent cases of children lost during the family-separation crisis of Trump's Zero Tolerance policy debacle drew a great deal of attention, it is in fact common for family members and lawyers not to be given enough information to locate detainees until it is too late and they have been moved to another facility in another state or deported.[30] Under President Obama, during an early iteration of crises in

Central American countries that brought a wave of unaccompanied minors to the United States, a family-detention facility was built in what clearly seemed to be a remote location that would be inaccessible to attorneys.[31]

Often, it is the most vulnerable people caught up in immigration enforcement webs who receive inadequate due process or none at all. Multiple studies by an independent commission of the federal government have shown how unreliable US procedures are for asylum seekers who come to the country pleading for protection from life-threatening circumstances. People who exercise their right to seek asylum in the United States must often wait for long periods of time just for their initial credible fear interviews, which determine whether they can make their full case to an immigration judge. When the interviews do happen, they are fraught with procedural problems. For one thing, they can be cursory to the point of making a mockery of the idea of a legal procedure. Some last only one minute.[32] Even if an asylum seeker can afford and find a lawyer to help them navigate the process, they can be denied access to that lawyer during the interview. Further, their lawyer can be denied the opportunity to participate even if present. Another long-standing problem is the coercion of people into signing statements that stipulate their own removal.[33] Asylum seekers are made to initial each page of a credible fear interview "transcript," often without any representation or even translation of the documents into their language.[34] (These transcripts are billed as verbatim even though they are *not* verbatim and differ from verbatim statements in ways that can make a material difference to an applicant's case.)

In some cases, they are intimidated or pressured into signing false statements that undermine their asylum claims because they have been separated from their children and are told that the only way they can protect their children is to sign a false transcript or an agreement to leave the country. These documents can later be used to impeach the applicant's testimony (with their coerced signature used as evidence that the "statement" is accurate, though whatever is contained in the statement often has not been translated into their language), which can in turn result in the denial of many legitimate asylum claims.

Whatever one thinks about unauthorized immigration, a system that fails to ensure basic due process for people ensnared in immigration courts or deportation proceedings is a system grossly indifferent to a foundational principle of any democratic country. We already know that some people in deportation proceedings are US citizens. Some get deported. Many mistakes are made, people's fundamental rights are denied, and the wrong people get deported because ICE so often is exempted from even basic judicial oversight.

Even the judges in immigration courts are sounding the alarm. They describe intense external pressure as well as challenges to their autonomy that often have the effect of allowing their superiors to decide their cases for them. The Department of Justice (DoJ) has imposed work speedups and case quotas that judges say prevent them from properly attending to the cases on their dockets. The DoJ has justified these requirements by referring to caseload backlogs, which are very real and quite well documented, even if they are not the result of immigration surges, as anti-immigrant rhetoric claims. In fact, a dearth of judges has stretched back for decades.[35] In 2019, cases were being scheduled out as far as 2023.[36] Every case any judge hears is unique and requires attention and focus. But immigration judges all over the country have complained that these speedups deprive them of the minimum time they need to hear their cases.[37]

The success rate of asylum seekers' credible fear appeals plummeted beginning in 2018 as the Trump administration imposed draconian expectations for reduced numbers of refugees and asylees.[38] One way the administration sought to achieve this was through a 2018 rule that all credible fear reviews "should be completed within seven (7) days of the initial determination by an asylum officer."[39] Like case-completion quotas, this kind of hastening virtually guarantees that legitimate claims will be rejected. More recently it has been proposed that the Pentagon take over some CBP functions and that military lawyers serve as immigration judges, even though immigration law is among the most challenging legal specializations and military lawyers are not trained in immigration law.[40] Attorney General William Barr has proposed "allowing judges to issue cursory opinions without explanation" to reduce the backlogs.[41] The union representing immigration judges has stated that they believe they could do their jobs more fairly if their courts were removed from the Department of Justice and made independent, as are bankruptcy courts.[42]

More generally, immigration courts are not set up to prioritize fair hearings. If you're picturing a standard judge, possibly in robes, seated in front of a courtroom, you're not imagining immigration court. Immigration judges are bureaucrats appointed by the Executive Office for Immigration Review (a part of the Department of Justice), not regular judges. The way the United States manages its immigration courts has been famously analogized by an immigration judge as akin to hearing death-penalty cases in a traffic-court setting.[43] As one immigration lawyer has said, "There's nowhere else in our system where the same branch of government can arrest, detain, charge, prosecute, review the case of, review the appeal of, have complete control of the custody of, and execute the sentence of the same person. There's a reason 'Kafka-esque' is tossed around so much in my world."[44]

The "courtrooms" in which these cases are heard are often just cameras and monitors. In 2019, closed tent courts were also erected in Brownsville and Laredo, Texas. Immigration cases are frequently heard via video conference, making communication very difficult. The ACLU has sued over this issue, documenting that it deprives clients of the ability to communicate privately with lawyers and to access translators. Studies show that people whose cases are heard via video hearings have a lower success rate.[45] Despite this, video is starting to replace live language translation as well, even though observers note that video translation is extremely difficult to understand.[46] While Jeff Sessions was serving as attorney general, he severely curtailed immigration judges' authority to postpone cases for purposes of allowing people time to find a lawyer or to obtain and prepare evidence to support their claims.[47] Sessions made clear he believed that immigration lawyers were conspiring to circumvent immigration laws, despite the fact that in many immigration proceedings the individual requiring representation has not broken any of those laws.

Each of these transformations of immigration proceedings has been initiated to take as much decision-making power as possible away from the judges who are trained to hear the cases. Their authority is being supplanted by a few powerful policymakers and influential lobbyists and advocates who are entirely outside the government but who share a vision of a whiter country and the opinion that anyone in immigration court deserves to be deported. A court system that cannot safeguard due process becomes powerless to check the advance of these policymakers and the agencies carrying their water, especially when the survival and growth of the agencies depend on detaining and deporting as many people as possible, often indiscriminately. These procedural shifts are all the more significant when ICE is flooding immigration courts, apparently without regard for whether the immigrants it is trying to deport pose any threat to anyone. As we will see, our current immigration enforcement policy has wrought this state of affairs.

—•—

IT IS A chilling paradox that due process is less robust for people in immigration proceedings than in almost any other kind of legal action, because the stakes are so high. Among the most terrifying actions that any government can take against a resident is to deport that person. In many cases, people who fight to receive asylum do so because deportation to their home country equals a death sentence. In other cases, people fighting deportation are US citizens caught up in Kafkaesque nightmares. ICE doesn't want us to see things this way, though. In fact, they don't want us to see much at all. We rarely see detained immigrants' faces or hear their stories, and ICE works hard to prevent us from seeing its prisons or video-camera kangaroo courts. ICE prefers that we picture deportees as faceless criminals being sent where they belong.

In order for ICE and CBP to justify their budgets and their power, it is important that they maintain the illusion that deportees are suspicious foreigners. But more often than people realize, neither is the case. Even during the Obama administration's shift to focusing on "felons not families" as targets for deportation, only around 12 percent of all deportees were found to have committed serious (level 1) offenses, according to ICE's own classifications of who constitutes a threat to public safety or national security.[48] This means the agency itself found that 88 percent of the people deported—during a time when the United States claimed it was focused on security as a deportation priority—posed no serious threat to public safety. Since the Trump administration has begun indiscriminate deportations, and even greater numbers of law-abiding individuals and families are being deported, that ratio is set to increase. In 2017, approximately 25 percent of the 143,470 ICE arrests (which for immigration purposes are a first step to deportation) were of people with no criminal convictions at all, and another 11 percent had no outstanding criminal charges. As we'll examine in more detail later, the creation of DHS and its immigration enforcement mandate were justified as responses to grave security threats. But DHS's immigration agencies don't fight crime, and we'll also see that they don't fight terrorism either.

Deportees usually aren't criminals, and sometimes they aren't even foreigners. As long as the US government has been engaged in deportations, it has deported US citizens alongside documented and undocumented immigrants. Sometimes all it takes to end up being deported is looking non-Anglo or having noncitizen family members. In early 2018, a Philadelphia native, Peter Sean Brown, was sentenced to be deported to Jamaica.[49] While in custody, he was verbally and physically abused by sheriffs guarding him while they waited for ICE to pick him up. Later that year, a US-born marine, Jilmar Ramos-Gomez, was imprisoned and put into deportation proceedings by ICE.[50] Sometimes, even whiteness is not enough to protect US citizens from being placed in deportation proceedings. Tracy Nuetzi spent a year fighting deportation proceedings despite having been a US citizen for sixty years, born to two US citizens who were living for a brief time in Canada.[51] Another US citizen, New York resident Davino Watson, was held by ICE for three years before being dumped, inexplicably, in Alabama.[52]

In these cases, the individuals held by ICE pending deportation managed to prove their citizenship, but others are less fortunate. Oscar Olivas, who was born and raised in the United

States, was deported to Mexico by CBP, who claimed he was not a US citizen after he applied to sponsor his noncitizen wife and stepchild. He had been living in Mexico, near the border, in order to commute to his job in the United States while his wife and her child awaited permission to live in the United States. To build its case, CBP threatened Olivas's mother with deportation and forced her to sign a pretyped declaration that his birth certificate was falsified. Once deported, because he was a US citizen and not a Mexican citizen, he was unable to legally obtain employment in Mexico, and his daughter, a US citizen, could not obtain proper school access. He had to fight the US government, which refused to acknowledge that he was clearly a US citizen, for reentry all the way to the Ninth Circuit Court of Appeals. The Ninth Circuit finally ruled that the burden of showing that Olivas was not a US citizen—that the documents he presented at the border were false or that there were none—belonged to CBP. A citizen should not be forced to fight for reentry to their own country, and none of us should have to fear that CBP or ICE agents will conspire to lie about the legitimacy of our passports, birth certificates, or other proof of citizenship.[53]

ICE agents have been known to blatantly lie in their efforts to initiate and complete deportations, and they have not always been disciplined for these violations. Ignacio Lanuza was nearly deported from the United States on the basis of a document ICE claimed he had signed in 2000 in which he agreed to voluntarily depart the country. Lanuza was eventually able to acquire a forensic examiner's report showing that the document had been forged by an ICE agent. The forgery was uncovered only because the agent referred to DHS in the document, despite the fact that DHS was created three years after the document was supposedly signed. But for that grossly nonsensical error, Lanuza would have been deported. However, the ICE agent at fault was never disciplined by ICE or DHS and continued to work for the agency until Lanuza successfully sued for damages, appealing an initial rejection of his claim.[54]

ICE also deports legal permanent residents. Right now an Albanian citizen whom ICE confused with someone else is fighting for reentry from Albania, where ICE deported him in 2018.[55] In some cases, errors have led to the deportation of people adopted by American families who fail to understand and properly execute the labyrinthine procedures required not just to legally adopt but also to change the citizenship of their children. Whether a child is automatically naturalized upon adoption depends on when that child was adopted. Sometimes adoptive parents fail to meet a deadline for a single crucial form they didn't know was required to complete the naturalization process for their child, and they miss the chance altogether. One Philadelphia woman discovered that her citizenship hadn't been acquired with her adoption when she was in the process of applying to become a member of that city's police force.[56] More recently, the adopted Korean-born daughter of a former lieutenant colonel in the US Army was told by DHS that there is no legal way for her to acquire citizenship or remain in the country because her parents missed a critical deadline due to her father's deployment. She will be deported as soon as her student visa runs out even though her adoption is fully legal and recognized by the US government.[57] Others make that discovery when they try to obtain passports, apply to go to college, or attempt other perfectly normal activities.

After someone is illegally deported they are likely to find it nearly impossible to reinstate their right to enter and live in the United States. It is difficult enough for many US citizens and legal residents to access the documents that immigration procedures (including citizen sponsorship of family members) require as proof of citizenship or legal residency when they are in-country. According to a 2006 survey by the Brennan Center for Justice at New York University, more than thirteen million US adults at that time did not possess proper documentation of citizenship.[58] Fewer than 46 percent of US citizens have a passport. The same survey also found that low-income citizens (those earning less than $25,000 a year) are more than two times as likely to lack proof of citizenship as more affluent citizens. Citizens in rural areas are similarly unlikely to have proof of citizenship. Birth certificates are currently the standard document to prove citizenship, but if they were replaced by a national ID card, as some hope will happen, the burden of acquiring official documents would increase, creating insurmountable bureaucratic hurdles to proving citizenship for some people. Low-income citizens in particular can end up terribly disadvantaged in the intimidating fight to prove citizenship because of the expense and time required for them to obtain the proper documents.

Fighting to prove your citizenship or legal residency from outside the United States is significantly more difficult than it would be inside the country. If a deported citizen is fortunate, and someone in the United States can advocate for them, they may have a chance to fight their way back into their own country. But that requires luck and resources that many lack. For a rising number of people, this has meant being torn from their families, communities, jobs, and homes.

—•—

IN SOME CASES, US citizens are being deported because of a secretive campaign to strip people of their citizenship. Denationalization is the act of entirely removing someone's citizenship and is one of the most extreme acts a state can take against an individual. It is the citizenship version of capital punishment, permanently ending a person's political self. For this reason, not only has it been fairly unusual, but many question whether it should ever happen. Denationalization was surprisingly common in the early years of the twentieth century. Between 1906 and 1970, 145,000 US citizens, both native born and naturalized, were stripped of their citizenship, some with no judicial procedures at all.[59] The last time the government attempted mass denationalization was during World War II, when the Roosevelt administration tried to purge the country of Japanese and Japanese American people. Such actions became much more difficult after the Supreme Court severely curtailed the circumstances under which citizenship can be eliminated.

But a subset of citizens, naturalized Americans, can be stripped of their citizenship, and United States Citizenship and Immigration Services (USCIS) has been targeting this group, looking for potential deportees to denaturalize. Seven percent of the US population is naturalized.[60] The ramp-up started slowly, around 1994, as a Republican Congress expressed skepticism about the foreign-born population more generally, and has accelerated recently. In the 1990s, fewer than twenty cases were filed in an average year. However, in 1997, the government audited more than a million records of individuals who were naturalized amid what was called the Citizenship USA campaign.[61] They found nearly five thousand cases of people who had been naturalized despite having disqualifying criminal records. The INS, based on its understanding of the Immigration Act of 1990,[62] claimed it had the right to revoke those naturalizations without court proceedings.[63]

Then the Obama administration initiated the secretive Operation Janus, which gathered data about naturalization applications with the intention of ferreting out people from "countries of concern" who had falsified their identity and thus secured citizenship fraudulently. The project was described as a counterterrorism measure after CBP discovered that 206 aliens from "special interest countries" who had received deportation orders had then reapplied and been granted citizenship under different names or birthdates. Under Trump, DHS and the DoJ have revivified Operation Janus and begun another related mission, Operation Second Look, to begin denaturalizing people—stripping them of their citizenship—regardless of whether they are from "countries of concern" or pose a threat to national security.[64]

From 2004 to 2016, an average of 46 denaturalization cases were filed each year. Between 2016 and 2018, prosecutors filed twice that number of cases per year.[65] Any denaturalizations are worrisome for those of us concerned with civil rights, but a sharp incline in denaturalizations should trouble anyone concerned with shadowy government practices that have grave consequences. Since 2017, after Trump took office, 107 denaturalization cases have been sent to the DoJ, and the administration currently states that it plans to refer about 1,600 cases.[66] In September 2017, DoJ filed its first three denaturalization lawsuits under Janus. Sixteen people were denaturalized in 2017, and USCIS data indicate that 2,536 naturalization cases have been targeted for in-depth review.[67] These numbers are expected to rise as ICE digitizes more fingerprints and uploads them to DHS's Automated Biometric Identification System (IDENT).[68] Indeed, according to DHS, over 700,000 files are pending review.[69] In 2019, DHS plans to spend more than $207 million for Operation Janus and a related green card fraud investigation.[70] ICE will hire three hundred new Homeland Security Investigations agents and additional staffers to focus on this work. Yet no evidence exists that any of these investigations are intended to or will uncover threats to US security.

Many of today's denaturalizations are not triggered by meaningful threats of fraud and may be unwarranted. Baljinder Singh, a naturalized citizen of twenty-six years, had his citizenship revoked under Operation Janus because he intentionally changed his first name on the application. Singh had been living an unremarkable life in New Jersey and was not charged with posing a threat to national security.[71] A Bangladeshi American had his citizenship revoked after it was discovered that he had reversed two letters in his name on his asylum application.[72] In another highly publicized case, Norma Borgono, a sixty-three-year-old grandmother from Miami, found her citizenship in jeopardy because of a crime she had committed before her application was granted and for which she had not been tried at the time of her application. USCIS and the Trump administration have taken her to court, even though she served her sentence and cooperated with federal investigators, on the premise that she intentionally lied in her application by concealing the fact that she had committed a crime.[73] Another naturalized American, Parvez Manzoor Khan, was accused of failing to disclose a deportation order that he had not known about and which was not clearly relevant to his application. During his proceedings he was denied access to translation services, and his lawyer was later disbarred.[74] The *New York Times* reported recently on mysterious, unexplained passport revocations near Detroit that shook the region's Yemeni American community starting in 2015.[75] No justification has been given for these first steps toward denaturalizing an entire group of people. It is difficult to see why so much effort is being expended on ruining ordinary citizens' lives.

Operation Janus and other denaturalization proceedings are so secretive that we don't know their entire scope or effects. But it is clear that DHS is investing resources in a long-term campaign to denaturalize people, and that like most of DHS's immigration work, this crusade is not a response to a national security threat. In the past, the government pursued only denaturalization cases involving misrepresentations of past serious crimes such as war crimes, human trafficking, or drug trafficking. But today, in an era when DHS is looking to denaturalize citizens, a naturalized citizen can never be entirely sure that simply living peaceably and minding their own business will guarantee their citizenship.

—•—

IN A COUNTRY founded to ensure individual liberty, under a Constitution expressly stating that no person—not just citizens, but all persons—should ever be taken into custody without cause or held at length without receiving due process, ICE's and CBP's practices and procedures fly in the face of our most fundamental legal principles. That reality makes those agencies a threat to everyone in the United States, citizen or noncitizen. Amazingly, the agencies are fully aware that they are eroding basic rights guaranteed by the Constitution. As revealed by the zeal with which they have fought lawsuits proving that their own agents were lying, they will work to hold onto or expand their unchecked power for as long as possible, in the face of ample evidence that their practices are corrupt.

A federal agency that permits or even encourages the forgery of documents purporting to prove that someone is deportable is an agency that threatens everyone in the United States. Ignacio Lanuza was able to fight his deportation. But it isn't difficult to imagine that a more adept forger than the ICE agent who was involved in Lanuza's case could create fraudulent documents that are more convincing, or could destroy authentic documents, thereby calling into question anyone's legal status. An agency whose employees can engage in this kind of fraud with impunity is a threat to the fundamental rights of all people in this country. Imagining that we are not a plausible target for ICE does not mean that ICE can't and won't come after us.

Slowly, often imperceptibly, US immigration enforcement has grown to encompass a massive, expensive, secretive web of agencies that routinely deprive people—immigrants and citizens—of basic civil rights and legal protections. Along the way, people are beaten, sexually assaulted, robbed, and denied compensation or justice. At the end of the process, thousands are thrown out of their homes and the country, regardless of whether they pose a threat to anyone's security or whether they have been law-abiding and contributing members of society.

CBP and ICE know that their agents and detention facilities are abusive. They are also aware that their field agents are incarcerating and sometimes even deporting US citizens. They know that their databases are riddled with errors that lead them to mistakenly target citizens and legal residents. They even have internal protocols for dealing with these kinds of errors, contradicting their own public statements that such things do not and cannot happen.[76] An ethical immigration enforcement apparatus would have cleaned house long ago. But both the incentives and the culture of the agencies militate against stemming the tide of abuse.

The law of the land is supposed to be just that: the law that applies to anyone within this land. This is a principle made explicit in the Fourteenth Amendment to the US Constitution, in which equal protection of the laws is guaranteed not just to citizens of the United States but to all persons in the United States. We should be alarmed if the core legal protections of our country—not just the frills and fringe benefits, but the most fundamental principles—deteriorate. When one branch of the government creates a legal black hole where even the courts' interpretations of laws and rights do not apply, we are all endangered. It is an ominous thing to let the basic rights of non-citizens erode—the rights that we claim belong to all humans, regardless of what their passport says. Agencies with the legal power to push property owners off their own land, to jail anyone suspected of lacking papers, to take citizenship away, to deport citizens, to kill people, and then to lie about it are agencies that erode the rule of law. In the absence of the rule of law, we will no longer have a democratic state.

If ICE and CBP are allowed to continue on their current path, the United States is only a short leap to a time when any citizen could hear a knock at their door and encounter uniformed officers on the other side who are ready to take their property and possibly their family into the custody of the US government. Or perhaps the government will look the other way as a private militia group targets us. If the person targeted is you, your lawyers and even your family members may be unable to find you, your identity documents may be rejected, someone could lie about your birthplace, and you could be held for a long time or even deported. Journalists may be intimidated out of investigating what happened to you. If you are imagining that this is something that happens to other people—people of a different race than yours, people with accents, people with criminal records, less educated people, poorer people—well, that's not necessarily true. And the longer our immigration enforcement agencies are allowed to expand their scope and persist in unlawful and dangerous practices, the fewer protections any of us will have. Noncitizens are canaries in democracy's coal mine. What happens to immigrants can and does happen to any of us. Regardless of what one thinks about immigration, one thing is clear: our current enforcement agencies have not earned our trust and do not achieve our goals—or much at all beyond enriching and empowering the people who work for them.

Although no good justification can be found for the ever-expanding flow of resources being poured into border control or the failure of authority figures to properly supervise how those resources are used, there is a story behind how and why this has happened. The chapters that follow will look at how these agencies were created, went rogue, and became such a grave threat to our rights and our safety. First, we'll examine how immigration has been handled and how US immigration law has developed over the past century, trends that have often been influenced by well-funded, well-organized groups and political actors with a white nationalist agenda. Then we will look at the current explosion of enforcement panic. In these stories, we can also find lessons and hope for a better way forward.

CHAPTER THREE

Inventing Illegality

IT IS TEMPTING TO IMAGINE THAT THE FRIGHTENING STATE OF IM-migration enforcement today is a flash in the pan—the momentary consequence of some factor or set of circumstances unique to contemporary politics that will dissipate in a few years. Maybe it's Trump? White working-class economic anxiety? Or it could go a little further back, to Tea Party nativist politicians and their supporters, like white nationalist congressman Steve King, who has openly spoken about the impossibility of "restor[ing] our civilization with someone else's babies" and has wondered out loud about how *white nationalism* and *white supremacist* became offensive terms.[1] Some may even think that the fault lies with the immigrants themselves, for coming to the United States in "wrong" ways, in large waves, or from "bad" places.

But the truth is that US immigration enforcement has been abusive and corrupt since its inception. As long as there have been people employed by the US government for the sole purpose of policing immigration, both at the border and in the interior of the country, those agents have broken laws, violated rights, ripped apart families, deported legal residents and US citizens, and continually reached for more power and more money than they could be trusted to use responsibly. In some cases they were carrying on deportation campaigns that civilians had been conducting, illegally but unsanctioned, before a US Border Patrol or interior enforcement existed. As we'll see, though, the country has never fully escaped the lawlessness of its earliest "law and order" immigration politics.

For immigrants' part, human migration is as old as humanity itself; it is absolutely inevitable, and attempts to stop immigration simply divert the paths of immigrants to new entry points. Immigration into the United States now is neither a crisis nor higher in proportion to the overall population than it was in earlier periods of immigration. Furthermore, today's immigrants aren't particularly different from previous generations of newcomers, despite what some nativists wish us to believe. Racist nativism isn't new either. Past influxes of immigrants also suffered contemptuous reactions from those who had arrived before them.

How did we reach a point at which very reasonable levels and forms of immigration are treated as a crisis and used to justify illegal enforcement practices? Before thousands of people could be employed for the purpose of hunting and deporting undocumented immigrants, there had to be laws that defined the border and the conditions under which it could be crossed. And before any purges, erosions of civil rights, immigrant prisons, or other abusive practices could take place, there had to be "illegal" immigrants to hunt down, lock up, and drive out.

The constant barrage of news we hear today about illegal border crossings, apprehensions, and ICE or CBP may make it seem as if the distinction between legal and illegal immigrants is long-standing, fixed, and legitimate. But neither America's founders nor the laws passed by many generations of congresspeople distinguished between "legal" and "illegal" immigration. The figure of the unlawful immigrant that has become a political lightning rod is a recent and intentionally crafted invention, designed in part to engineer the composition of the population and in part to generate and channel specific types of fear and anger for political purposes. Examining the very beginnings of the invention of "illegal" immigration will help us sort through what happened once alarm bells were sounded that this phenomenon was on the rise and needed to be rooted out, and how we ended up creating a shadow paramilitary police force dispersed throughout the country and empowered to take actions no other law-enforcement agents are permitted to take.

"Illegal" or "undocumented" immigrants weren't invented by a line in the sand or a wall around the country. They came into being through the enactment of laws that make some immigration legal and some illegal. It is in those laws, not a specific place where one country begins and another ends, that the country's borders can be found. National boundaries are not visible even when you are standing right on them. If you find this hard to believe, consider the misguided stunt of Congressman Duncan Hunter, who in 2019 claimed to cross a section of the US border as a way of showing that it is inadequately fortified. After he drew the media attention that he sought, someone pointed out that Hunter and his wife were under indictment for campaign-finance fraud and were not permitted to leave the United States. In fact, though, he had not violated the terms of his plea: he was seventy-five to one hundred feet from the legal boundary of the country, at a vehicle barrier, a fact that was later used to embarrass him.[2] But in this sense, national borders aren't that different from private property. It isn't always clear precisely where your property ends and where your neighbor's begins unless there is a dispute over something such as a pipe on one side that leaks onto the other side. Laws will determine how the two properties can be demarcated and what the consequences of any particular type of breach should be. The property line itself only exists in a meaningful way if those laws recognize the boundary, if someone enforces the laws, and if we agree that the laws and enforcers have legitimate authority.

The way we go about carving our border is linked to the purpose we want it to serve. Borders can be used to ward off security threats, retain human capital, and prevent the movement of illicit substances, among many other goals. Believe it or not, these were all reasons that Mexico sought to enforce its border with the United States in the mid-twentieth century, often pleading for US cooperation.[3] The US border, which has shifted considerably over time, was not used to keep immigrants out of the country until the late nineteenth century. In fact, for most of this country's history, the United States prioritized the need for settlers and workers so emphatically that it tried to ensure that as many people as possible immigrated to the country and did its best to attract people who wanted to stay. Leaders speaking about immigration referred to desirable immigrants who wanted to become citizens as "intentioners" because they had intentions of becoming citizens rather than simply wanting to stay for a bit, make some money, and then return to their country of origin.[4] The idea that we would try to keep most potential immigrants from entering the United States, or that we would use the border to accomplish this goal, is less than a hundred years old.

What does it mean to invent the particular kind of national border that makes some forms of immigration illegal and some immigrants undocumented, and what purpose does such a border serve? Making immigration illegal isn't the same thing as keeping people out, of course. To make something illegal is to use law to forbid it and to create a punishment that is imposed on people who break the law. The laws don't prevent the thing from happening. If they did, no one would speed on the highway. The border that makes people's presence "illegal" by creating penalties for undocumented entry consists of a set of laws that determine who can enter the country under which circumstances and that penalize those who break the laws. It is these laws—which invent visas and green cards, determine penalties for lacking papers, and designate agencies to enforce the penalties—that make some immigration illegal.

That the border is an invention of law, and not a place, is a truth accepted by both pro- and anti-immigration factions. Anti-immigration activists believe that getting rid of legal penalties for undocumented immigration would give us open borders. If we don't enforce the law, we don't have a border, they say. Pro-immigration advocates believe that the laws criminalizing immigration and immigrants are unnecessary legislative choices that have unfairly denied law-abiding workers and families the protection of a country where they live and work. Neither side considers the border to be a line on the map; for both, it is the laws that create the border.

Another surprising point of agreement between anti-immigrant and pro-immigrant forces is that the laws that invented illegal immigration in the United States were brought into being by elite lobbying organizations and interest groups for the purpose of restoring a white nation and for ethnic purification. To put it starkly, the criminalization of undocumented immigration and subsequent harsh enforcement practices were the products of long-term advocacy by white nationalists—many of whom were political and social elites—who openly decried the immigration of nonwhite people to the United States and who glorified the idea of a white nation. We know that the original architects of the idea of undocumented immigration wanted to use immigration policy to whiten the nation because they were quite transparent about their belief in white racial supremacy and in advocating for extreme measures to achieve as white a population as possible. And we know they sought to maintain the elite credentials of the movement because they spoke openly about the legitimacy that came with having highly educated and polished advocates.

These leaders and their interest groups saw white nationalism as both a goal and a selling point of immigration restriction. They were proudly open about their commitment to a vision of a US population made up of people from the original nations who sent settlers to the colonies and early republic: the only true, white Americans. They wanted to preserve "native stock," which they defined not as "persons born in the United States" but as "persons who descended from the white population of the United States at the time of the nation's founding."[5] At the margins, they disagreed about who really counted. The strictest nativists sought a citizenry of Anglo-Saxon origin. Others disagreed. Madison Grant, a powerful, old-money, elite-educated blue blood who dedicated himself to "race science," believed that we were a Nordic country.[6] Grant was an unapologetic white supremacist and advocate of eugenics whose arguments were praised by Presidents Coolidge and Harding.[7] In either case, however, these were people who wanted primarily to ensure that the United States rid itself of members of races who they believed were biologically and culturally unable to become good citizens. In addition to restricting immigration, many sought to ensure a better, purer future population through sterilization programs for members of "undesirable" races.[8]

The laws these men succeeded in supporting and passing were informed by faux scientific theories of racial hierarchy and whiteness that were popular at the time but fell out of favor. According to the theories, Irish, Italians, Poles, Russians, and Jews all made up distinct and distinctly inferior races that were infecting the superior gene pool that predated their arrival. It may be hard for our twenty-first-century minds to imagine that what we now refer to as ethnicities or nationalities—if we think about them at all—were considered races. But not only were they considered races; they were considered deficient and undesirable races, and definitively different from the white race. If any of these early twentieth-century definitions of whiteness were used today, they would reclassify all but a few US citizens as nonwhite.

The laws that grew out of this anti-immigrant activism and its definitions of whiteness started popping up in 1917 and culminated in extensive immigration legislation in 1924.[9] Both the laws and the racist motivations behind them were embraced by millions of Americans who had been recruited to the cause of nativism. Well-educated social and political elites elicited and stoked ordinary people's fears of strangers, of the different and the unfamiliar, and of potential losses of safety, property, or status, They projected those fears onto the bodies of new immigrants and then crafted policies to "protect" Americans from the concocted threat. These lawmakers and lobbyists invoked law and order when it suited them, but they were unworried primarily about law and order; when either law or order got in the way of their goals, they were perfectly willing to ignore both.

PRIOR TO THE twentieth century, two things were true of immigration to the United States that are no longer true: First, there was little federal regulation of either immigration or the border. States were charged with creating and enforcing what regulation did exist, and those regulations varied from state to state. Rules about who could move between the states mattered as much as rules about who could come through ports of entry that allowed non-Americans into US territory, and they were rooted largely in racially motivated interests in controlling the movement of slaves and free black persons.

Second, deportations were not systematic in the country's first two centuries, although when they did happen they were brutal and sometimes deadly. In the earliest days of the republic, the Alien and Sedition Acts made deportation possible on political bases, and laws such as "poor laws" called for the deportation of paupers. But these laws didn't lead to mass deportations or many removals at all. Later, there were periodic calls to remove people considered too poor to support themselves (often referred to as "public charges"), as well as sick, mentally deficient, or racially undesirable people. For example, very poor Irish individuals and families were deported throughout the nineteenth century.[10] In other cases, the unwanted were simply moved from one town or state to another. Ships responsible for transporting immigrants to this country were sometimes forced to return passengers to their country of origin if they were deemed unsuitable for entry. Most notably, in the nineteenth century mass executions were carried out against Mexican-born people living in parts of the

Southwest that had been claimed by the United States.[11] But there was no coordinated large-scale national effort to prevent immigration or deport immigrants. In fact, prior to 1890, proportionate to their numbers, few immigrants were ever deported by the US government. And at the same time that these events were occurring, immigration was considered necessary and was encouraged, even if some specific immigrants or groups of immigrants were unwelcome and were subjected to abuse. Systematic ongoing mass deportation requires a lot of funding, concerted political will, and a coordinated enforcement apparatus[12]—a combination of factors that didn't exist until very recently.

It was nativist suspicion and fears about Chinese immigrants that initially spurred the US federal government to assume more responsibility for regulating entry into the country and for using this power in a way that was explicitly racist. These fears built over a period of decades in the late nineteenth century. Chinese immigrants were accused of lacking morality, taking jobs from Americans, infecting the native-born labor force with bad habits such as smoking opium, and other baseless claims. A wave of virulent anti-Asian sentiment that led to a rash of racist state and local laws, and even violent riots in some cities and towns, peaked in 1882 when Congress passed the Chinese Exclusion Act. This law placed a ten-year ban on the entry into the United States of people from China. Chinese nationals already living in the United States found their status uncertain as well. Ultimately, the act was extended several times, and it wasn't officially repealed until 1943.

For many people, Chinese Exclusion marks the first point at which illegality could be conceived, in part because of the ban itself and in part because the ban precipitated the development of a bureaucracy and of authorization documents to prove that one's presence in the country was legal. These had not previously existed. But the possibility for undocumented immigration on a mass scale didn't yet exist. We were still a nation of relatively open borders for large numbers of people who wanted to come here.

US openness began to change in dramatic fashion at the turn of the twentieth century when an influential set of groups inspired by spurious "scientific" theories of racial superiority began beating the drum of nativist fears about how immigrants from undesirable ethnic stock could pollute the US workforce and population. In 1911 Congress set aside what was at the time an enormous, unprecedented amount of money—$1 million—to apply "cutting-edge" social science to the study of immigrant ethnicities. Social "scientists" of the time claimed to be able to predict rates of criminality, mental illness, low intelligence, and other unfavorable traits based on craniometry and phrenology—the study of skull sizes and shapes. They also made patently unsupported demographic claims, for example that recently arrived immigrants had lower rates of assimilation than immigrants who had been settled longer.

Techniques such as early twentieth-century phrenology, craniometry, and scientific racism, or "race science," were used to justify a push for measures to "protect" the good stock of Americans of northern European ancestry from the "inferior" people of eastern and southern Europe. Scientific racism was some of the earliest social science ever practiced. In the United States, race scientists almost always considered themselves to be white, and they prioritized whiteness; they were dedicated to collecting observations and data they could use to generalize about which groups of people constituted races and what their characteristics were, and to construct a hierarchy of races. We now regard all of this to be junk science. Skull shape isn't useful for predicting much beyond hat size, and social scientists have authoritatively shown that immigrants incorporate and assimilate over time with little variation based on where they come from.[13] But as we'll see in Chapter 4, white nationalists are still using junk race science to influence immigration policy today.

Race science gave rise to a variety of efforts designed to perfect the population through ethnic purification, eugenic sterilization laws, pronatalist policies that encouraged white women to have more children, and other racialized laws. It is worth noting, as an aside, that staunch eugenicists and their work contributed to eugenics laws that were used to accomplish things like forced sterilizations of girls believed to be promiscuous or "feeble-minded" (in the language of the time). Eugenics laws passed in the United States became the model for Nazi eugenics laws, and their American authors were invited to Germany, where they received prizes and praise for their role in the pioneering of eugenics legislation.

Eugenicists weren't just tucked away in ivory-tower social science departments. They also occupied the nation's most prominent offices. President Woodrow Wilson vocally supported both nativism and eugenics. Of the immigration wave in the early twentieth century he said, "But now there came multitudes of men of the lowest class from the south of Italy and men of the meaner sort out of Hungary and Poland . . . [with] neither skill nor energy nor any initiative of quick intelligence."[14] Although Wilson did not want to close US borders, he made no secret of the fact that he didn't think all immigrants enhanced the existing population of the country. Of this "race problem" he claimed, "The whole question is one of assimilation of diverse races. We cannot make a homogenous population out of people who do not blend with the Caucasian race. . . . Oriental coolieism will give us another race problem to solve, and surely we have had our lesson."[15] Wilson was one of the first politicians to popularize the phrase "America First" as a way of insisting that immigrants could not have hyphenated identities and needed to be able to Americanize if they were to stay.[16] The KKK adopted the phrase as well, as a way to offer strong support for Wilson's nativist instincts.

Perhaps even more powerful than President Wilson was the network of influential white nationalists who formed eugenic anti-immigrant interest groups. Members of some of the nation's most elite families, many of whom were Ivy League graduates, joined forces in associations like the Immigration Restriction League and the American Protective Association. These groups lobbied for restrictions and populated Congress with their members to help their cause: preventing the immigration of the southern and eastern European immigrants whom they viewed as less valuable, and possibly less human, than their own kind. Republican senator Henry Cabot Lodge said in an address to Congress:

> More precious even than forms of government are the mental and moral qualities which make what we call our race . . . they are exposed to but a single danger, and that is by changing the quality of our race and citizenship through the wholesale infusion of races whose traditions and inheritances, whose thoughts and whose beliefs are wholly alien to ours, and with whom we have never assimilated or even been associated in the past.[17]

Irish, Italians, Russians, Polish, and many other Europeans were referred to as "contagions" that could infect the good stock of Americans tracing their lineage to countries like England. If you are a current US citizen whose grandparents were born in the United States, the chances are high that you are a descendent of these so-called contagions. But, of course, today white nationalism has new targets in its crosshairs.

In 1924, these patrician white nationalists got their way and at the same time inadvertently sowed the seeds of the "crisis" of undocumented immigration that we face today. The Immigration Act of 1924, often referred to as the National Origins Act, virtually halted immigration from almost all the countries from which immigrants were coming to the United States at the time. It imposed quotas to enact the dominant view of the moment: that anyone who wasn't of "original settler" extraction was racially distinct from and inferior to members of founding nationalities. Through the use of these racial quotas, people of almost all nationalities, except northern Europeans—mostly English—became instantly ineligible to come to the United States. Senator Albert Johnson, one of two cosponsors of the legislation, justified the law by saying, "Our capacity to maintain our cherished institutions stands diluted by a stream of alien blood, with all its inherited misconceptions respecting the relationships of the governing power to the governed."[18] His cosponsor, the Princeton-educated senator David Reed, thought the immigrants coming to this country were analogous to the barbarian invaders that had taken down Rome.[19] Another supporter proclaimed, "The greatest menace to the Republic today is the open door it affords to the ignorant hordes from Eastern and Southern Europe, whose lawlessness flourishes and civilization is ebbing into barbarism."[20]

The goal of the law was twofold. First, it sought to ensure that the American citizenry would look like the citizenry of colonial times. It simultaneously enforced a dubious but powerful definition of Americanness: that "real" Americans are white Americans. Aspiring immigrants from pariah countries had to be kept out at all costs, prevented from having children (when possible), and discouraged from marrying "real" white people or sullying the white gene pool with mixed-race children. Even Scandinavians, whom we now often point to as classically midwestern settlers bearing the attributes of traditional Americans (and who I noted had defenders), were seen by some as ethnically undesirable. Congress set the quotas using the 1890 census to create benchmarks for allowing immigration from countries that had sent early settlers to the United States, and halting it from European nations whose residents were not considered white. Some congressmen even called for using the 1790 census, to ensure the ethnically purest quotas.

The white nationalists who tried to close the border were impassioned, but they were not strategic. At least three major oversights in the legislation created conditions that undermined their intentions, ultimately yielding the exact opposite of what they sought. The long-term result of their effort to close the border in 1924 was not a white nation exercising strict control over who enters the country. Instead, they ensured that white citizens would be outnumbered by nonwhite persons.

Their first oversight was a weak documentation system and a lack of provision for punishments that could be applied to people who didn't have documentation. How could a law be enforced if no punishment was specified for breaking that law? At the time, the United States didn't have a well-established visa system to make it possible to distinguish between people who had arrived in accordance with the quotas and those who had circumvented them. Few documentation requirements were in place before the quotas were imposed, and those that were on the books had long been frequently ignored because they served no purpose.[21] An official act requiring the possession of a visa had been part of an immigration bill passed in 1917. Immigrants were also supposed to be issued a certificate that created a record of their arrival and admission.[22] However, the use of these documents was erratic, and often documents were only provided once someone was going through the formal process of naturalizing and becoming a citizen.[23] The law created an identification card for non-US citizens, a precursor to today's green card, given to anyone admitted for permanent residence. But this was not a robust visa and documentation system, because the country still lacked adequate infrastructure for implementing and enforcing such a system. It had only just become illegal for US citizens to travel internationally without a passport, as part of a 1918 Wartime Measure Act, and keeping track of entry and exit paperwork was not yet fully systematized. This meant that some people were still entering without proper papers, and others with proper papers did not get properly logged.[24] There were also people who had arrived prior to 1924 but had evaded inspection by immigration officials and who now had no way to obtain proper papers. In addition, prior to the quotas, many people had formally declared to their inspector that they were coming to the United States for a visit but later decided to stay, rendering their original declarations legally false.[25] These misrepresentations had not widely been considered particularly problematic, in part because at the time, the act of staying in the country was regarded as a sign of commitment and good citizenly character. Finally, some people became undocumented because they left the country temporarily, thinking they had the right to return, but then encountered bureaucratic and legal problems when they sought reentry.

Anyone whose arrival suffered from irregularities, whether they were accidental, the result of a bureaucratic error, or intentional, could not get the ID card that the National Origins Act required. In large part this laxity was possible because there seemed to be an official consensus that almost no one had been sneaking into the country undetected.[26] That would soon change. After the act went into effect, people's lack of documentation—especially that of immigrants who simply had not been properly logged—became a problem, not just logistically but in the eyes of Congress, as we will see. So did the absence of penalties for being undocumented.

The second oversight had momentous consequences: The law did not ban immigration from anywhere in the American continents, including Mexico. Not everyone thought this omission was a good idea, but those who believed that it was and that it would not undermine the overall goal of whitening the population won the day. Indeed, some Europeans who were denied direct entry evaded the rules by coming into the United States through Canada.[27] After the act went into effect, Mexican citizens were still eligible to come to the United States. To some of the most fervid proponents of white racial purity, this was a source of disappointment. It certainly was consequential.

Third, no plan was put in place to determine how the jobs that were traditionally performed by the very newest and poorest immigrants would be done. A significant population of Mexican and Mexican American people already resided in the country in light of a previous failure of Congress to plan around the labor market; one effect of the implementation of Chinese Exclusion during a period in which there was high demand for labor had been that the immigrant workforce quickly came to rely on increasing numbers of Mexican nationals. Often these Mexican laborers were given only temporary permission to stay in the United States.[28] Many were more than happy to leave their home country because the chaos arising from the revolution that had unfolded there between 1910 and 1920 remained unresolved, but not all of them intended to or did stay in the United States.[29] And prior to the 1924 law, immigration inspectors had focused disproportionately on excluding Chinese workers coming through ports, allowing others to enter without being detected.[30] The number of Mexicans in the United States ticked upward after 1924 as European immigrants became unable to enter the country in large numbers.

In the early years after the National Origins Act passed, immigration officials were left to improvise solutions to these problems. They exercised a great deal of discretion at the border in many towns and at specific checkpoints. Officers employed to check documents recognized some of the people who repeatedly crossed back and forth over the border, as people had been doing so at the southern border for as long as it had existed, and found ways to accommodate them. Sometimes they issued discretionary temporary travel waivers and border-crossing cards for short-term visitors and workers who needed to travel within ten miles of the border but who were not qualified to settle in the United States after 1917.[31]

Eventually, Congress institutionalized short-term work visas to address some of the specific labor shortages and needs that cropped up after 1924. A large proportion of these went to Mexican workers, leading eventually to more formal short-term programs that followed in the 1930s and 1940s. The most infamous of these programs was the brutally exploitive Bracero Program, which brought Mexican workers into the United States to do agricultural work starting in 1942, and the H-2 program, begun in 1943 to bring in Caribbean workers to cut sugarcane in Florida. The Bracero Program was described as legalized slavery by Lee Williams, the secretary of labor who oversaw its conclusion in 1964. The H-2 program, not much better, was the predecessor to today's H-2A temporary agricultural-worker program and its sibling, the H-2B program for unskilled workers in nonagricultural sectors. Each later iteration of temporary work program brought people into the country for limited periods, generally with the expectation that their employers would be responsible for returning them. But the "importation of workers" on either discretionary or formal short-term visas inevitably led to the presence of people who came here to work without having acquired visas, because they either didn't qualify, didn't know they needed to, or found it easier to carry on without them. And what all the programs had in common was that some people overstayed their short-term permission and became, to use language that barely even existed at the time, "illegal" residents. This way of becoming undocumented has become so prevalent in recent years that now much of the new undocumented population is made up of people who overstayed a visa, which is not in and of itself a crime.[32]

The failure of Congress to forbid immigration from the Americas in combination with ongoing labor market needs and confusion over documentation meant that the long-term effects of closing off legal immigration were the exact opposite of what the laws intended. But even in the short term, problems with the new documentation requirements were immediately evident.

At first, some of the chaos surrounding the legal status of immigrants who lacked the newly mandated immigration paperwork could be mitigated by a legal provision that now seems extraordinary. When the quotas went into effect, a statute of limitations governed irregular entry. After five years of otherwise law-abiding residence, immigrants who were unable to document their legal entry (either because their documentation had been lost or because they never had proper papers) became legal residents, although not citizens.[33] Eventually the residency-period requirement was reduced to three years.[34]

We should pause to take note of this remarkable fact, because it will become so pivotal later in the narrative and because it tells us something very important about what it really means to forbid undocumented immigration. A statute of limitations creates a countdown clock toward a point at which a society's legal system says legal consequences can no longer be attached to past conduct. In the United States, statutes of limitations exist for most infractions. Most but not all statutes of limitations are set at the state level and vary from state to state. Only the most heinous crimes—murder, for example—

have no statutes of limitations. The first two decades of the twentieth century comprised a period in which massive support gathered for openly racist immigration restrictions. Many members of the country's political elite as well as masses of their constituents wanted to purge the country of anyone who wasn't of settler extraction. Both racism and nativism ran rampant. Foreign-born persons of Asian descent were simply ineligible to become citizens. And yet a statute of limitations on any kind of consequence—incarceration, deportation, or fines—allowed many people who lived in the United States for a period of years to permanently shed their undocumentedness. For all the virulent racism that motivated the purges and restrictions, it was still seen as better for this country to incorporate someone who had arrived without a visa than to have a class of the permanently undocumented. Becoming a country in which masses of people lived their lives in perpetual limbo was antithetical to our self-understanding as *a nation of citizens.*

The statute of limitations on irregular immigration was not merely a relic of a prenativist time, nor was it in peril after the quotas went into effect. Despite the explosion of nativism that had led to the National Origins Act, policymakers took an approach to the presence of undocumented persons that was equal parts pragmatic and humane. Although legislators had an interest in excluding and deporting "undesirable" immigrants and in preventing the reentry of anyone who was removed, they still hoped to attract and retain "desirable" immigrants. To do any of these things, the country needed a better system of documenting who was arriving. Policymakers and many immigrants shared an interest in solving this problem.

—·—

THE 1924 LAW had banned most immigration, but we cannot say it made immigration fully illegal because it established no penalties or punishments for entering or being in the country in defiance of the quotas. Because the nation lacked a documentation system equipped to distinguish between those who were and were not welcome, discussions about immigration legislation continued directly after the passage of the 1924 law and persisted for several years. To complete the invention of "illegal" immigration, the United States now needed penalties to enforce, a documentation system to identify targets for enforcement, and enforcement personnel to do the work of penalizing and removing violators.

In 1929 Congress took up the questions of both penalties and documentation. The issue of penalties was fairly straightforward. The law that was passed, the Registry Act of 1929, created penalties for those who arrived without paperwork after the quota system was put in place.[35] It said that a person who was found to have entered without authorization could be subject to a year in prison, and reentry for those who had been previously deported was considered a felony punishable by up to two years in prison.[36] These penalties completed the process begun in 1924 when limits were first placed on immigration. After passage of the 1929 law, there were consequences that could be enforced for unauthorized entry or presence. The new stringency was implemented by paperwork requirements. Noncitizens planning to stay in the United States needed to file a declaration of intention (also called "first papers"), which was made before a court and indicated a person's intent to become a citizen. Their declaration had to be accompanied by a "registry record," also known as a "certificate of arrival." Previously the record of arrival had not been required, which makes sense for a country that treated most of the people arriving and most of the ways they arrived as equally legitimate and lawful. The requirement changes considerably tightened up the US system of documentation by making it easier to distinguish between lawfully and unlawfully present people. Along with imposing a penalty for unlawful presence, it was now possible to call some immigrants "illegal" and punish them for being so.

The second part of the bill, which was essentially a circumscribed amnesty for undocumented immigrants, was more complicated. Even though the penalties portion of the act acknowledged and tried to shore up the country's weak immigration documentation requirements, some people had already managed to become undocumented under the weak system, as we know. The Registry Act created a new, even more generous statute of limitations to ensure that they did not remain a permanent underclass.

The appeals that motivated Congress to write the "amnesty" portion of the bill will sound familiar to anyone who has listened to pleas on behalf of undocumented immigrants in any era. One congressman read a colleague's letter that reflected the sentiments of many:

> *May I urge a favorable consideration on the part of your committee to the proposal to give relief to over a million law-abiding residents of the United States who through technical omissions are prevented from becoming naturalized American citizens?*
>
> *In some instances, the fault is that of the Government rather than the individual. Let me illustrate by citing a case which has recently come to my attention. . . . A young man from my district came into the country in August [1907] from Canada, with his parents. He was a child of three or four years at the time of his entry. He was educated in the public schools of Massachusetts, a high school, and is a preparatory-school graduate, he has lived every day since his entry into the country in Massachusetts. He has a good Job and is a respected young man.*
>
> *Yet he cannot become a citizen without leaving the country and reentering simply because the Government failed to record his entrance back in 1907. He is only one of many who came in without record in the days when we did not check up arrivals as closely as we do to-day.*
>
> *Is it fair to these men and women to prevent them from becoming citizens of a country which is their permanent home, when they own property, and are rearing native-born American citizens? Is it a good policy for the Government itself to forbid them the right of citizenship?*[37]

The Registry Act allowed these and related circumstances to be smoothed over rather than turning them into original sins from which an immigrant could never recover, as is current practice. The act set forth both the new rules about regularizing undocumented immigrants and the updated documentation requirements. We call those provisions "registry."

At first, the Registry Act only permitted "regularization" for anyone who was otherwise eligible for citizenship (persons born in any Asian country, for example, were ineligible at that time) if they (1) had entered the country before June 1921, (2) had resided continuously in the United States since entering, (3) had good moral character, and (4) were not subject to deportation. As a letter read by one member of Congress involved in the law's passage indicated, Congress believed that the act would apply to up to one million people living in the country.[38] Even with the 1921 deadline, which would later be advanced, this was not a minor amnesty.

Importantly, the Registry Act made no distinction between an "irregularity" caused by the immigrant (e.g., through evading immigration officials) and one caused by poor bookkeeping on US officials' part. The intentional and unintentional undocumented immigrants were treated the same way.

Not everyone supported this kind of rolling amnesty, to be sure. A minority on the Committee of Immigration and Naturalization protested that the proposed law effectively forgave all irregular entrants whose first act upon arriving was to violate the immigration laws of the United States.[39] But the Registry Act not only passed; it endured and was renewed for six decades following its passage. Unlike the National Origins Act, it has never been repealed. Every renewal advanced the "arrived by" date, allowing new generations of immigrants to avail themselves of the grace that once characterized our nation's approach to enforcement. Each renewal discussion reaffirmed one abiding principle of US citizenship: long-term residents who have not impugned their own moral character, regardless of the age at which they arrived or any irregularity in their legal status, deserve citizenship and are desirable citizens. This rationale, which would be reiterated each time the act was renewed and the registry date advanced, evinces a principle that is deeply important to American citizenship practices. It is the same principle we've always used to deal with immigrants becoming citizens, all the way back to the nation's First Uniform Rule of Naturalization (1790): immigrants become citizens by living and working in the country. For almost all the immigrants who came, no act of original sin—not even an undocumented entry or the overstay of a visa—could nullify the processes that take place as a person intertwines their life with the lives of other citizens and the nation.

Even in an era of rampant white nationalism and nativism, US legislators showed compassion for the innocent, unwitting, and truly committed aspiring citizens who were caught up in the legal web of still-nascent immigration rules. But they weren't just compassionate; they were also practical. They knew that looking the other way or criminalizing undocumented people by blocking their pathway to citizenship would only lead to more severe problems down the road.

Registry remains on the books to this day, but the current "entered by" date (1972) has been stalled for decades. In the chapters that follow, we'll look more closely at what happened to registry through the years and what we could do with it today.

By the 1930s the nation's immigration apparatus was emerging. We had restrictions, documentation requirements, and punishments for undocumented persons. There were sweeping new laws to enforce. All that remained was to actually enforce them. But that was no small task.

CHAPTER FOUR

Enforcing the Border

BEFORE THE 1924 QUOTAS WERE ENACTED, THE UNITED STATES had no federal border patrol agency and no other well-established means for policing either its land border or the immigration documents of people already living in the interior of the country. The Bureau of Immigration had stepped up enforcement a bit after 1918, as passport requirements and other rules went into effect. But an official federal Border Patrol was not created until 1924. It started with just a few hundred employees, the vast majority of whom were deployed in Texas.

The creation of a border patrol to seal off the country to people who might try to violate the National Origins Act or flout the 1929 documentation requirements proved difficult for reasons that remain vexing even today. From the outset, what few resources the Border Patrol had were concentrated on the southern border, where the Washington bureaucrats who were invested in controlling immigration also sought more control of the frequently unruly citizen population. But circumstances on the border did not lend themselves to effective policing by the federal government. The borderlands have always been too vast and forbidding a landscape to patrol effectively. This problem was particularly acute in an era when much of that patrolling was done on horseback, but even after those guarding the border acquired a squad of Chevrolets, it remained an overwhelming space to monitor. And much of the region had only been in US possession since the US-Mexico War of 1846–1848, rendering the affiliations of its very diverse residents quite complicated.

Trying to change the social and economic environment of areas where people lived and worked was even more problematic. America's borderland towns were geographically, culturally, economically, and politically worlds away from the country's capital, where illegal immigration was being defined and where anger about immigration was being stoked. Generations of residents in the region, both north and south of the border, were deeply invested in their unique way of life. They had nothing to gain and a lot to lose from the imposition of border-crossing restrictions and a daily routine involving armed guards and police patrols. In fact, many residents of borderland towns still feel this way, and for this reason many detest CBP checkpoints[1] and have fought to prevent the building of barriers and a wall.[2]

The rhythms of work and of life at the border did not and still do not comport with the bureaucratic categories and de-limitations that policymakers sought to impose. In many cases these towns predated the border that had been drawn around or even through them and that continued to shift as the United States pushed westward. Residents of the towns—and of the expanses of desert and ranch land between them—had little use for policing who entered and left and even less patience with meddling Washington legislators.

A porous border enabled workers, business owners, tourists, and goods to move back and forth between countries with ease. The opportunity for Mexican and American workers and their families, as well as Japanese and Chinese merchants, to efficiently travel between the two countries was a critical feature of US borderland economies and communities both before and after the 1924 law went into effect.[3] By the 1920s, 98 percent of the agricultural workforce in southern Texas was Mexican.[4] Farmers pushed back very hard against attempts by the Border Patrol to prevent free movement of the workers they depended on. In fact, US farmers remained so depen-dent on the large numbers of skilled and reliable workers from Mexico that, later, the Mexican government would sometimes be more motivated than many in the United States to keep Mexican workers from coming to this country.[5]

A fluid border was of vital importance not only to Ameri-cans and their businesses but to an array of foreign countries and companies. Most residents of towns near the border benefited from an informal free-trade zone.[6] Tourism alone had created a boom for people living near the border, as Americans enjoyed going to places like Tijuana to gamble, drink, and indulge in other vices.[7] Once there, they crossed in both directions with relative ease, benefiting the economy on both sides. People also crossed the border to escape the strictures of Prohibition, which had been instituted in 1920.[8] Borderland communities argued that Mexico's omission from the 1924 quotas was proof of the exceptional status of free movement in the Southwest and that any change to that status would undermine lucrative trade and good relations with Mexico.[9]

No one who benefited from the special status and way of life that had developed in the borderlands wanted to destroy those privileges by sealing the border. This isn't to say that the borderlands were magically free of the nativism that infected the rest of the country. That was hardly the case. Residents and officially sanctioned law-enforcement agents like the Texas Rangers participated in periodic deportations, some of which were brutally violent, and carried out gruesome lynchings against Mexican and Mexican American people. For the people engaged in aggressive campaigns against Mexicans and Mexican Americans in the Southwest, lynchings, illegal deportations, and other atrocities served to enforce racial hierarchies in the context of concerns about not only white supremacy but also sovereignty and citizenship.[10] This is the legacy inherited by the civilian border patrol militias of the present. But borderland nativists shared little common ground with the pseudoscience-embracing, blue-blooded, Harvard-educated members of the Immigration Restriction League and other eugenicist groups that had pushed the 1924 legislation. And they had many reasons to be suspicious of intrusions from Congress and the distant East Coast establishment figures it represented. The distrust was mutual. In fact, as we'll see, elite nativists in the 1980s and 1990s sought to distance themselves from rougher, nonelite nativists, emphasizing their university degrees and other legitimizing credentials to gain the trust of Americans who weren't sure what to think about immigration.

For a long time, borderland residents were able to remain free of extensive federal intrusion. Congress provided little direction to Border Patrol in the early years.[11] Until documentation penalties were created in 1929, borderland towns from California to Texas were largely on their own when it came to immigration, as they preferred. This independence didn't vanish quickly; it proved difficult to manage the border from afar. Immigration figures for the time back this up, showing that the effect of the 1924 legislation was hardly immediate. As described in the discussion in Chapter 3 of the National Origins Act, some in Washington were uneasy about this fact, and particularly about Mexican immigration, which remained unrestricted by the 1924 law. However, proponents of limiting immigration from Mexico had failed to compel Congress to include that country in the quotas. If nativists wanted to keep out Mexicans, they were going to have to rely on the enforcement of laws requiring papers and documentation as well as a more muscular and wide-ranging policing agency than had ever existed before.

At the time, nativists combined forces with people who wanted a borderland "vice squad" of sorts to enforce morality provisions such as Prohibition and antiprostitution laws. The proponents of such a squad were not primarily interested in catching people sneaking across a border or in kicking anyone out. They believed, often correctly, that gambling, prostitution, and the illicit sale or consumption of alcohol thrived in this comparatively lawless part of the country that was still in many ways the "Wild West," and that the immoral behavior needed to be reined in. Thus, the very earliest version of a border patrol was mobilized in large part as a vice squad.[12] Immigration concerns became a pretext for the deployment of law enforcement to an area of the country that had long evaded the grasp of moralizers in Washington. The early border police did enforce immigration laws, occasionally rounding up and removing residents, often violently and with little respect for the rights of the people they were deporting. But initially they had neither the personnel nor the budget to be capable of the frequent, large-scale, organized purges that Ivy League eugenicists sought and would later pursue with zeal.

Perhaps because the work was so exceptionally tough and offered meager rewards, the new, official Border Patrol was staffed by rough men from its outset. Early on, it was so hard to attract officers that supervisors were forced to ignore the congressional requirement that agents pass a civil service exam.[13] Many were ex–Texas Rangers, the group founded to extract land from Mexican and indigenous people occupying parts of the Southwest that were taken from Mexico and to hunt down runaway slaves.[14] The Rangers, known for their violence, had a reputation for lynching, among other brutal acts. Administrators advertised for "strong men," attracting cowboys and trigger-happy adventurers who sometimes joined forces with the very bootleggers and law breakers they were supposed to target for prosecution and removal.[15] Even though many moralizers wanted a patrol to root out vice, most recruits were not ideal candidates for honorably discharging vice-squad duties. Officers were found drunk on the job, driving recklessly, and taking bribes.[16] Border patrol work did and still does attract a fair number of rogues, people whose character is suspect and whose qualifications are sparse. Exacerbating this unfortunate facet of CBP culture is the fact that all the US border-protection agencies that have existed since the 1920s have shared an indifference to rooting out the scoundrels among their own ranks. To this day, abuses of authority by border patrol officers represent one of the least-reported vulnerabilities of this country's border-protection system.

In addition to a general lack of interest in policing its own employees, Border Patrol early on carved out for itself exceptions to the restrictions that applied to other law-enforcement agencies. First, in 1925, Congress quietly exempted it from requiring warrants for searches, seizures, and arrests.[17] From its earliest days, then, Border Patrol was freed from the Fourth Amendment restrictions that limit the searches and seizures that police and other law-enforcement officers can pursue. This exceptional interpretation of the highest law of the land did not change in 1933, when the Immigration and Naturalization Service (INS) was created to manage Border Patrol, the Bureau of Immigration, and the Bureau of Naturalization. These new agencies handled an array of tasks related to immigration,

including bureaucratic processing and so-called Americaniza-
tion efforts, which encouraged learning English and adopting
what were deemed standard American cultural practices. At
the time it was conceived, the INS was a part of the Department
of Labor. Although arguments have been made that an agency
charged with the responsibilities of both welcoming new citizens and enforcing immigration law has the potential to be
more humane than an agency like ICE, which is essentially a
deportation agency, INS was drawn into enforcement from the
outset. In part this happened because INS was created in an era
when legal immigration was as limited as it has ever been in
US history. But even when the INS found itself unable to fund
direct deportation, it was responsible for outsourcing deportation work to state and local officials. Some speculate that ultimately this facilitated the development of expedited removal
techniques that more efficiently deported people.[18]

From the early years after enforcement penalties were created, skeptics suspected that the exceptional understanding
of the Fourth Amendment that Congress had carved out for
Border Patrol was dangerous. Leaders including Secretary of
Labor Frances Perkins and the head of the newly created INS,
Daniel MacCormack, fought to shape the scope and reach of
Border Patrol activities.[19] They believed that immigration enforcement's early lawlessness was an ominous sign and sought
to rein it in. Perkins and MacCormack worried about abuses,
and they also wanted to ensure that Border Patrol's power was
focused where it could be used for its stated purpose—enforcing
immigration laws near the border—instead of being dissipated

as agents were allowed to roam farther into the interior of the United States and engage in practices that weren't directly related to immigration. They worked together to address concerns about INS's more extreme practices, implementing reforms to safeguard due process in the adjudication and administration of immigration cases. One such reform was a directive in 1933 that prohibited warrantless arrests except in cases where an INS officer actually observed the person crossing the border. Other reforms sought to help so-called hardship cases, in which people had established a residence, started or married into a family, and perhaps lived in the United States for a long time. Like the practice of registry, these reforms took as a widely held truth that someone who had put down roots in the United States deserved to stay here.

Perkins's and MacCormack's changes to INS proved a major stumbling block for those who wanted a more muscular and less constrained Border Patrol. One such figure, Border Patrol's El Paso district director Grover C. Wilmoth, took a leading role in consolidating the power of the agency in the face of challenges and constraints. As a border militarist, Wilmoth in the 1940s became an influential voice in Washington. He encouraged two insidious practices: mass raids (called "roundups") and "chain deportation," the use of informants and interrogation of apprehended immigrants to find others.[20] He also sought to eliminate existing procedural hurdles to executing deportations.

As Wilmoth lobbied to broaden Border Patrol's powers, agents pursued mass deportations and regularly ignored the laws designed to constrain their actions and the boundaries within which they could act. Such practices continued throughout the 1930s and early 1940s. The exemption from Fourth Amendment requirements for probable cause was supposed to apply only to people crossing land and sea borders, at the point of inspection. Border Patrol officials insisted that this restriction prevented them from properly doing their job and were well aware that patrol officers frequently disregarded it.[21]

As recounted in Deborah Kang's richly descriptive history of the INS, *The INS on the Line:*

Wilmoth and [Border Patrol supervisor Willard F.] Kelly sought to license what they themselves characterized as questionable practices. . . . As Kelly stated, "[patrol] officers' authority to stop vehicles promiscuously on the highways leading away from the border has been questioned innumerable times, yet we have continued to act without proper authority." Even though the Border Patrol statute stipulated minimal standards for car searches (Border Patrol officers had to have some reason to believe that the vehicle was transporting undocumented immigrants), Kelly admitted that in practice, Border Patrol officers stopped cars with little or no discrimination:

As you are aware, our methods of operation have been such during the past ten years, and from the period between 1924 and 1931, that in no one case out of one hundred could our officers show reasonable cause to

believe that the vehicles they stop contain aliens who
are being brought into the United States.[22]

The solution, as they saw it, was not to bring the agents into
line. Instead, they thought Congress should change the law so
that their illegal practices were made legal. Rather than insist
that officers document a reasonable cause for any stop they initiated, Kelly sought a legislative amendment that would sanction standing procedures. As Kelly described the procedure,
"The actual practice for years has been for Border Patrol Units
established at strategic points on highways leading away from
the International boundaries (at some points as remote as 100
miles or more from the boundary), to stop and inspect all traffic coming from the direction of the border." Under the policy,
the Border Patrol estimated that officers stopped an average of
3,323,488 motorists per year.[23]

It took some time, but eventually they succeeded. In 1946
Congress passed Public Law 613, which allowed Border Patrol
to execute warrantless searches and seizures in the interior of
the country and not just at fixed border checkpoints.[24] The
law stated that Border Patrol agents could search within the
territory, without the same meaningful limits or supervision
to which any other law-enforcement agent would be subject.
The law also explicitly gave INS officers the power "to board
and search for aliens any vessel within the territorial waters of
the United States, railway car, aircraft, conveyance, or vehicle,
within a reasonable distance from any external boundary of the
United States"—to address Border Patrol's concern that people

evaded apprehension at the border and then disappeared into border communities as workers or otherwise took refuge. "Reasonable distance" was defined by district directors of the agency as one hundred miles. This is the origin of the hundred-mile zone, within which border-protection agents are not held to constitutional standards that all other law-enforcement agents must meet and can arrest people without reasonable cause. The INS also permitted district directors to request an expansion of the zone on a district-by-district basis.[25] And Border Patrol officers still had the (self-proclaimed) authority to make arrests without warrants beyond the hundred-mile zone, though they would need to assert reasonable cause.

In the 1930s and 1940s, Border Patrol still lacked the resources to reach deep into the interior of the country. It sometimes struggled with budget and personnel shortfalls. For example, in 1943 Border Patrol apprehended roughly sixteen thousand immigrants. In 1944, it was directed to "completely secure" the border, which it estimated would mean apprehending three hundred thousand people; yet the agency employed a hundred fewer officers than it had the year before due to staff reductions and the challenges of training, equipping, and housing agents.[26] Still, the framework for a powerful and unrestrained agency was slowly coming into existence.

Border Patrol's conduct during raids and deportations continued to be lawless in ways that should have immediately alarmed agency heads and triggered disciplinary actions. In the 1930s and 1940s, some raids deported groups that were equal parts US citizens and noncitizens. Things ramped up dramatically in the 1940s, as new, superficially less violent but much more insidious methods came into use. In McAllen, Texas, a single raid resulted in the deportation of almost seven thousand people.[27] From Los Angeles to Detroit to many other areas of the country, federal, state, and local law-enforcement agents—with the cooperation of private employees of organizations such as hospitals—would descend on parks, workplaces, and other areas, where they searched for anyone who looked non-Anglo. In particular, they targeted individuals who looked Hispanic, indigenous, or Asian, with little or no regard for their legal status or rights. Sick people were abandoned on stretchers at the border.[28] Men, women, and children were transported to and dumped in areas outside the country where they had no access to food or water. The death toll for large roundup campaigns could number in the hundreds. Victims were deported with no warning and no due process.

Border Patrol's actions became even more brutal in the 1950s, when they instituted humiliating policies like strip searches and mandatory head shaving to intimidate and mark undocumented immigrants.[29] Border Patrol insisted on distinguishing "criminal aliens" and began to intimate that criminality was of particular concern among undocumented immigrants.[30] Things came to a head with Operation Wetback, conducted in 1954 under the authority of the Eisenhower administration, which swept up over a million people in one year. As the name suggests, Operation Wetback was explicitly and intentionally racist, targeting Mexican and Central American residents of the United States. All over the country, masses of people, both immigrants and citizens, were herded like cattle onto buses, trains, and planes. Once kicked out of the country, Operation Wetback victims were left to fend for themselves. Some of these Americans, including children as young as five, were never able to gain reentry. Usually, getting home required the kindness of a contact in the United States who could secure proof of legal residency. Others had to return surreptitiously, taking great risks to reunite with their families.[31] Much as is the case today, through a 1996 program that drafts state and local law enforcement into the federal government's immigration enforcement efforts,[32] programs existed at the time to allow the federal government to offer support to state-level enforcement agencies.

Operation Wetback remains one of the most vicious ethnic-cleansing efforts in the country's history. It left in its wake both broken families and furious farm and business owners who were deprived of their workforce. It has been pointed to as evidence that Trump's plans for mass deportation will fail in solving the real problems of the US immigration system.[33]

To compensate for Border Patrol's inadequate infrastructure—for example, the fact that it lacked detention facilities to incarcerate everyone it rounded up pending deportation—the agency also outlined mass voluntary departure procedures, which 2008 presidential candidate Mitt Romney would later unsuccessfully promote as "self-deportation." When even these measures failed to achieve the desired result, Border Patrol leadership found new ways to circumvent the law, directing officers to forgo keeping written records so they could focus more of their time on physical removal.[34]

The significance of immigration enforcement lawlessness grew during the 1940s and 1950s as guest-worker recruitment mushroomed in response to the labor shortages caused by a closed immigration system (recall the aforementioned Bracero Program and the H-2A visas). In some cases the government hoped that guest-worker programs would take pressure off detention facilities for immigrants caught by the Border Patrol, which were overflowing and inadequate to the task they had been assigned.[35] Detention was (and still is) spoken of as a deterrent to undocumented immigration but has never succeeded in this goal.

In the 1940s, the climate also changed, bringing into focus the country's multifaceted commitment to seeing itself as a white nation and its willingness to use citizenship status to achieve this aim. In 1942, President Roosevelt issued Executive Order 9066, creating a War Relocation Authority to strip Japanese Americans of their property and incarcerate them in detention camps, effectively nullifying their citizenship. Through the power of the Renunciation Act of 1944, Japanese Americans were given loyalty questionnaires, and many were pressured to cede their US passports and nationality and deport themselves to Japan. The hostile policies toward Japanese and Japanese American persons, which treated over seventy thousand citizens and legal residents in America as aliens, persisted for the duration of World War II. Five thousand Japanese Americans serving in the US military had their citizenship revoked. The government also arrested thousands of Germans and Italians under the authority of the Alien Enemies Act, but most were not detained for an extended period or subject to a denationalization campaign. Earl Warren, then attorney general of California, expressed the nativism driving the attacks on the citizenship of Japanese Americans: "We believe that when we are dealing with the Caucasian race we have methods that will test the loyalty of them. . . . But when we deal with the Japanese we are in an entirely different field and cannot form any opinion that we believe to be sound."[36]

The US Supreme Court sanctioned Japanese internment in two cases from 1943 and 1944, Hirabayashi v. United States and Korematsu v. United States, which upheld the curfews. *Korematsu* was only disavowed by the Court very recently, in the same controversial decision that regrettably approved Trump's "Muslim Ban."[37]

At the same time that the Roosevelt administration was targeting persons of Japanese descent for denationalization, however, it took a more generous turn with respect to undocumented immigrants. In 1940, the Nationality Act advanced the registry deadline date to 1924, allowing anyone who had entered the country by that point to become a legal resident, or, as lawyers and policymakers say, to "regularize" their status. This was an extension of just a few years, but it signaled that registry remained an important part of the country's immigration apparatus.[38] The government's rationale for changing the date reveals a consistent commitment to the idea that longtime residents ought to become citizens:

> This would include a number of aliens of good moral character, who have resided in the United States for more than

10 years, and are not subject to deportation, but who cannot proceed toward naturalization because of a lack of a sufficient record of arrival. It is not in the best interests of the United States that there should be a considerable number of aliens here who have resided in this country for many years and who are otherwise eligible for naturalization and anxious to become citizens, but who are prevented from doing so because of the absence of a record.[39]

Records show no significant pushback in Congress against the modest update initiated by the executive branch. The overriding goal of those advocating a restrictive approach was to exclude "anarchistic or other subversive groups."[40] It appears that the "good moral character" requirement—understood at the time to screen out those with suspect political views—was sufficient to blunt potential criticisms of the registry date advancement.

—•—

AND SO WERE created the structural conditions for today's harsh, racialized, and often lawless approach to immigration. In the 1920s, Congress and a set of elite white nationalists erected the nation's first barrier to immigration. They established a border not with fencing but with laws that imposed penalties on those found to have entered the country without authorization, without proper documentation, or in direct violation of new quota laws. They also created agencies empowered and funded to interpret and enforce those laws unrestrained by the principles and procedures that guided law enforcement in other realms.

The border still wasn't a place or a thing one could look for in Texas or Arizona. But now it was embodied in legislation negotiated and enacted in Washington and enforced, at first quite sporadically, through an agency with some money and power but very little supervision. This border was not built with bricks or sighted on a map by surveyors; it was a slow legislative improvisation on the part of influencers and policymakers whose main goal was keeping the US population as white as possible.

Once a legal border to immigration had been created, the country needed persuading that unauthorized entry was something they should care about, and that the newly invented figure of the unauthorized immigrant was someone to fear, someone worth spending a lot of resources to deport. It wasn't a foregone conclusion that a campaign to stir up fear and resentment against immigrants would work. After all, lots of conspiracy theories fail to inspire mass movements and the sacrifices they require. But without such a movement, there would be no money for a militarized border wall, no excuse for muscular enforcement agencies to intrude into our private lives and property, no justification for ballooning personnel, detention, and equipment budgets, and, critically, no outlet for nativist rage.

As anyone who has tried to create a law, or even a budget for a small family household, will tell you, it is virtually impossible to predict all the possible ways that outside forces will interact with one's decisions. In the case of the 1924 National Origins Act, its authors failed to anticipate that their new prohibitions would starve the labor market, thus encouraging immigrants who were no whiter than the immigrants the quotas had barred. By the time they moved to act against this trend with a Border Patrol, the die had already been cast. Undocumented immigrants were finding their way into the country, especially via the hard-to-police southern border. Once in place, the pathways for surreptitious entry became entrenched as the information needed to use them spread. Ultimately this would mean that less and less immigration to the United States would originate in white, or even European, countries.

The consequences of creating a border zone with a legal reach that stretched deep into the interior of a vast country, of allowing the enforcers to break laws, and of giving license to an enforcement-at-all-costs approach in which the Fourth Amendment was at best an afterthought remain with us. This insidious way of thinking and the enforcement apparatus it engendered endured through the enactment of a new set of immigration laws that we'll explore in the next chapter, and then metastasized starting in the mid-1990s.

CHAPTER FIVE

Two Steps Forward

PASSING THE NATIONAL ORIGINS ACT, CREATING DOCUMENTA-
tion requirements and punishments for irregular migration,
and deploying a border patrol to enforce those laws did not
give America's immigration restrictionists the white nation
they sought. Paradoxically, their efforts ensured that the United
States would become home to millions more nonwhite people
than before. By 1960, the percentage of the US population that
was foreign-born had decreased by 40 percent from 1924 levels. But within that decline, one number was on the rise: The
number of people in the United States who had been born in
Mexico and other Latin American countries had more than
doubled. Europeans were being kept out, but Mexican and
other Latin American people—immigrants and guest workers

filling holes in the labor market—were coming at higher rates than in the past. Overall, people who came from Mexico and Latin America were a quickly growing percentage of the immigrant population in the United States, a fact that would prove consequential as the country transformed its immigration laws in the middle of the century.

The imposition of new documentation requirements in 1929, in a country that lacked the infrastructure to seal off all its land borders or even properly inspect everyone who was arriving, had all but guaranteed that there would perpetually be undocumented people living in the United States. This meant that immigration remained on the mind of legislators through World War II and the start of the Cold War. Exacerbating this effect was the fact that for the first time in US history, the country undertook formal provisions to admit refugees. These went into effect in 1948 under the Displaced Persons Act, targeting not the Jews displaced by World War II but primarily people fleeing Communism. In fact, the way in which the Displaced Persons Act was structured made it very difficult for displaced Jews to enter the country.[1] Daniel Tichenor wrote of the bill, "Nativist legislators no longer spoke plainly of the racial inferiority of particular groups, as they had before the war, but the ethnic and racial targets of exclusion remained unmistakable."[2] Still, immense demand existed for entry visas to the United States, and the Displaced Persons Act, in combination with an update to the law in 1950, brought four hundred thousand people to the United States, many of whom would not have qualified under the 1924 quotas.

In 1952 Congress passed further legislation in the form of the McCarran-Walter Act. Like the National Origins Act, McCarran-Walter was driven by immigration reports requested by congressional committees that very clearly expressed the racialized and nativist fears of nonwhite immigration.[3] The bill's cosponsors were like-minded restrictionists, but by 1952 they faced a more robust opposition, not just from Democratic members of Congress like Emanuel Celler and Peter Rodino, but also from President Truman. They structured the legislation to preserve racialized quotas but added rules that prioritized work skills and family reunification within those quotas. In addition, they capitalized on Cold War fears to create new bars on immigrants identified as ideological enemies and nonconformists.[4] Congressman Francis Walter, who presented the legislation as maintaining the quotas, later acknowledged that in fact it was an enhancement of the racialized restrictions.[5] The bill was a failure for everyone in the sense that it both reiterated a US commitment to racialized immigration hierarchies by maintaining limitations on the immigrants that the 1924 act had restricted and also included loopholes that, while clearly intended *not* to change the ethnic makeup of incoming immigrants, had that very effect. Significantly, McCarran-Walter made possible the entry of Mexican workers who were considered "returnable."[6] As became obvious later, not everyone who entered on a temporary basis decided to leave after their visa expired.

Critics of McCarran-Walter decried it as a more politely worded paean to racial hierarchies, going so far as to remind their fellow congressmen that US racial codes had been the model for Nazi laws.[7] Shortly after the legislation went into effect, in 1958, Congress attempted to directly address the "problem" of the undocumented by updating the Registry Act. The initial Registry Act date, which permitted "regularization" of any immigrant who had entered the country before June 1921, was now too far in the past to help the numerous longtime undocumented residents who had arrived after that date, many of whom were lodging pleas for regularization that had to be considered individually.[8] A Senate report on the issue stated:

> In view of the diminishing potential of aliens eligible to seek benefits under section 249 of the Immigration and Nationality Act, it is believed an amendment of this section to extend the date of required entry and enlarge the scope of authority to permit discretionary consideration of the adjustment of status of aliens who are subject to deportation on generally technical grounds only would be justified.[9]

The proposed amendment not only advanced the registry date but also modified the criteria for using the Registry Act. Anyone who had entered the country by June 1940 became eligible to regularize. In addition, the law eliminated the requirement that anyone seeking to use registry not have a deportation order for having committed a crime. This eased life for a segment of the immigrant population, particularly for people whose deportation orders stemmed from dubious "crimes" such as breaking laws forbidding the distribution of foreign language publications and other similarly nativist measures that had been passed to enhance the homogenizing social effects of the National Origins Act. Instead, after 1958, a person seeking to make their immigration status "regular" (i.e., documented instead of undocumented) simply had to show that they were not guilty of a felony, smuggling, or subversive political behavior.[10]

A letter from the Department of Justice to the Judiciary Committee, which was printed in both the Senate and House reports, expressed the Eisenhower administration's support for regularization of long-term residents.[11] Though the white nationalism that had informed both immigration policy and enforcement efforts had not abated, there was also widespread recognition that people who had lived and worked in the country for long periods deserved and needed to be citizens. Decades had passed, allowing the assimilation of the many European immigrants who had not been considered desirable aspiring citizens when the National Origins Act was enacted. By the 1960s, a traditional pattern of generational incorporation had brought the Irish, Scandinavian, and eastern and southern Europeans who were not seen as "white" in 1924 into the country's ever-changing definition of whiteness. And as the civil rights movement achieved successes, a new political milieu was being forged by proponents of more egalitarian policies. These factors led President Johnson to successfully demand from Congress what Eisenhower and Kennedy had been unable to extract: an entirely new immigration policy that in many ways was intended to, and did, move the United States beyond its explicitly racialized immigration laws. The 1965 Hart-Celler Immigration and Nationality Act (INA), which passed with a great deal of support in Congress, has been adjusted through the decades, but it remains the framework for today's immigration system.

On the surface, the INA appears to be diametrically opposed to the quota system in spirit. Its effects have most certainly been to rapidly and thoroughly dismantle the limits that existed on immigration between the 1920s and the 1960s. It initiated an enduring openness to immigrants and immigration that not only restored some permeability to the country's borders but laid out principles that had remained unarticulated in the immigration laws of the nineteenth century. The bill opened up immigration, allowing immigrants from all countries to come to the United States in large numbers. Instead of ill-founded science propounding unproven racial hierarchies, its authors referenced more respectable criteria such as skilled work qualifications and family connections in the United States.[12]

But just beneath the surface, the change happening was complicated and less progressive than it seemed. The impulse to liberalize was real, but fears about nonwhite immigration had not so much disappeared as they had evolved in the four decades since imposition of the quotas. Parts of the Hart-Celler bill were influenced by men who still wanted to preserve a white nation, albeit one in which Europeans were now generally thought of as white. Explicitly racist arguments were becoming less socially acceptable by the time the bill was being debated, a fact that nativist activists noted and incorporated into their strategies going forward.[13] But racism, racial anxiety, and a pull to keep the ethnic makeup of the population as it was or to prevent specific racial outcomes were still present. Senators from Texas, Arkansas, Florida, and North Carolina all expressed open skepticism about the provisions that would allow people from Asia and Africa to immigrate to the United States. Senator McClellan of Arkansas actually worried that the bill would exacerbate the violence and riots taking place in cities with large African American populations that were chafing under the legacy of Jim Crow. An expert witness argued strenuously against introducing "new seed" to the United States.[14] Senator Edward Kennedy, who was floor manager for the bill, promised of the new legislation, "It will not upset the ethnic mix of our society."[15]

One faction of congressmen that was skeptical about non-white immigration thought that prioritizing workers through high-skilled employment visas would be a sound immigration policy and could simultaneously serve to filter out nonwhite immigrants. Another faction, led by a congressman named Michael Feighan, thought that allowing existing Americans to sponsor relatives would lead to a naturally self-perpetuating ethnic makeup of the immigrant population. Those who wanted to pass the bill responded not by extolling the contributions that Asian and African immigrants could make to the country but by offering reassurances that the racial makeup of the immigrant population would remain largely as it had always been. The two factions compromised on a three-tier priority system that privileged family reunification and skilled work. Refuge, not previously encoded in immigration law, was third.[16] This priority system has been transformative: in the contemporary era, two-thirds of all immigrants to the United States each year arrive via family sponsorship.

Like the racially charged immigration quotas of 1924, family reunification was intended to ensure that immigrants to the country would be people who Americans thought were white, at least by the standards of the time. But because the authors of the legislation failed to understand how the country's demographics were shifting, they would end up achieving the reverse, just as their predecessors in 1924 had done. Nonwhite immigrants from countries like Mexico and the Dominican Republic, who had already come to the country when European worker migration was halted, were soon followed by refugees from Cambodia and Vietnam and by the first sizable numbers of legal immigrants from other Asian and African countries. All of these people were eligible to sponsor children, parents, spouses, and siblings (but only those relations; more distant relatives such as grandparents and cousins were ineligible) to come to the country, and they did so, engaging in what is sometimes called "chain migration."

Family reunification is a source of intense frustration for contemporary white nationalists who yearn for the America they imagine existed in the 1950s. Despite the fact that there are caps on most types of visas, and years- or decades-long delays exist for almost all forms of family reunification, critics believe that family reunification creates a loophole through which too many immigrants—especially nonwhite ones—can enter the United States. This grossly misrepresents how family reunification works. The backlogs for most of these categories are decades long. A Mexican person seeking to bring their adult child to the United States this year would have needed to file more than twenty-one years ago; a Philippine-born person trying to sponsor a sibling today would have needed to file twenty-three years ago. More distant relatives like aunts and cousins are ineligible for family reunification.

Nor do the economic arguments that family reunification has been bad for the country hold up to scrutiny. In fact, family reunification passes the costs of immigrant integration to the families and communities that sponsor immigrants. In countries with purely skills-based immigration "points systems," for example Canada, integration requires substantial government resources and support. In family reunification systems, relatives must show that they have sufficient income to support the immediate relatives they are permitted to sponsor, and they can be held responsible if the people they sponsor use certain social-safety-net resources. There are many other costs that the family reunification system lodges with family members rather than government programs. The social capital that families and members of coethnic communities make available to newly arrived members whom they sponsor is an important determining factor in the speed of assimilation and the degree of success the immigrants are able to achieve. Families and ethnic communities offer help with unfamiliar bureaucracies, transitional language skills, immediate housing, and emotional support, along with financial and other resources essential to moving and obtaining employment. But for people who want control over the racial makeup of the population, or who are inclined to favor the principles of white nationalism, family reunification is a threat.

The new immigration law opened up the possibility of immigration to the United States to many who had long been excluded. But in the decades prior to its passage, some of those who had been legally excluded had immigrated to the country anyway, and they remained undocumented. Congress acknowledged this state of affairs by updating the registry date again, advancing the "entered by" date to June 1948 in the same session in which it passed the new INA. The discussion prior to the update's passage of who merited the privilege of regularization continued to emphasize the importance of a person's ties to country and community that had developed over time, and reflected a keen awareness of how difficult and unfair it was to have to "live in the shadows," to use a contemporary phrase, without proper legal status. Testimony given to Congress repeatedly stressed the general themes articulated in the statement below, delivered on behalf of the national professional association for immigration lawyers (known as the Immigration Bar) by Edward Dubroff:[17]

We have, I would say, many people in limbo, in immigration limbo, who have arrived subsequent to June 28, 1940, and prior to December 24, 1952, who, by reason of certain exclusions contained in our other statutes, cannot qualify for suspension of deportation, adjustment of status, and so forth. I believe this registry provision which began, as I recall, on June 28, 1940, was a part of the Alien Registration Act of 1940, [and] has proved a very workable provision[,] and that these people who deserve adjustment, who have been here physically and continuously all this time . . . far too many people are relegated to the role of hiding out. . . .

It is no advantage to this country to have such persons in limbo, in the United States for all possible purposes, but unable to call this their country and unable to take part in the affairs of this country.[18]

The testimony of those who resisted advancing the registry date reflected a confusion about whether doing so helped criminals: "We don't know who that section of the law embraces. We don't know who is in this country today where amending that particular section of the law would grant them every opportunity for citizenship. It would take care of the dope peddlers. It would take care of the smugglers. It would take care of all the conceivably bad elements that are in existence in the country today."[19]

In fact, criminals were not eligible to apply for legal status under the Registry Act. It is notable that those who objected to updating the registry date were not simply opposed wholesale to a statute of limitations on the crime of undocumented entry or presence; they were concerned only that a few bad apples might end up in the barrel. Undocumented entry was not yet perceived to be an original sin from which a person could never recover. And the concerns of the few skeptics were both answered and overridden by proponents who emphasized the retention of the good-moral-character requirement, which made it possible to weed out people with criminal records or those who didn't seem sufficiently civic in their INS interview.

The legislative discussions clearly and powerfully articulated the distinct dilemma of people who were technically deportable but were also clearly committed and desirable aspiring citizens. As one member of Congress stated:

> By changing the date . . . the law would establish the date of entry as prior to the effective date of the Immigration and Nationality Act, the present basic code. In other words, a benefit would be granted to persons who entered this country before the new requirements which became effective at that time. No harm would result to this country from the enactment of this proposal. On the contrary, it would serve to permit the reuniting of families and to permit technically deportable aliens to remain in this country without harshly tearing them away from the arms of their loved ones here.[20]

In 1965, the proposition of regularizing long-term residents was not especially controversial. There was no fierce debate over advancing the date. The White House supported the measure. Indeed, the administration's letter in support of the legislation, which contained detailed policy recommendations on other matters (including other issues related to registration), did not even touch on, let alone question, whether to advance the registry date.[21] The INS commissioner, Raymond Farrell, also supported the advancement of the registry date based on the principles of long-term residence, as shown in this colloquy with Congressman Michael Feighan:

Mr. Farrell: I believe, sir, that it would be very helpful if we could now move that date up, because, also, many of these people are married and they have families, and they have established themselves as good members of the community, and to deport them would be cruel. It would be very helpful if that date could, also, be moved up.

Mr. Feighan: Mr. Commissioner, you understand that there are several cases which involve only illegal entry where the man has been here for 20 years.

Mr. Farrell: Yes sir.

Mr. Feighan: And is married and has raised a family here. The record shows that he and his family have been good law-abiding people and the deportation of the father, aside from the fact that his homeland is under Communist occupation, would be as you say, a pretty cruel act and an unreasonable act and this is the kind of case I had in mind in my original inquiry. What remedy could we authorize in a case like this without opening the gates for undesirables or for other abuses?

Mr. Farrell: Well, sir, I think that if we could establish that they are of good character for a sufficient period of time, and if we could, also, establish that they are not Communists or Communist sympathizers, that we could do a great good if we could move that law up—move the date of the law up, because many of them have been here, as you indicate, 20 years—some of them have been here 15, 17 years, and I am thinking of specific cases and they have established themselves in the community . . . [T]hey are good people [in] many instances, and I think that that law would be helpful.[22]

This exchange reveals deep and abiding ideological bigotry of a sort that has always been present in American politics. And we know that Feighan was unsupportive of making the United States a more racially diverse nation than it already was. But also evident is empathy and even openness to undocumented immigrants who had slowly become Americans as they lived out their lives in this country.

The willingness of people who were skeptical of changing the racial composition of the US population to acknowledge the citizenizing effects of time-in-residence on undocumented immigrants has all but vanished. Where did that understanding go? The answer to this question can be found in a campaign not unlike the one that led to the 1924 restrictions. A small, militant group of highly educated and affluent activists went to work on policymakers and the public, drilling home the message that immigrants were likely to be criminals, terrorists, and freeloaders. It didn't begin immediately, and it took years of work to build the widespread resistance to immigration, particularly undocumented immigration, that animates the political Right today. For a long time these activists achieved few legislative victories, and they racked up stinging losses. But, eventually, they succeeded.

CHAPTER SIX

Two Steps Back

IN THE YEARS IMMEDIATELY FOLLOWING THE PASSAGE OF THE NEW
INA through the 1970s, the ethnic composition of the foreign-
born population of the United States changed. While the eastern and southern Europeans that had been rejected in the 1920s
for not being white enough were now generally considered
white, they no longer sought to come to the United States in the
numbers that they had earlier in the century. Instead, waves
of refugees—people fleeing war and Communist repression—
from Southeast Asia were arriving, some with permission and
some without. (Refugees and immigrants are legally distinct
categories. In the past, some US legislation has included refugees in the overall total numbers of annual immigration
permitted. Currently, however, refugees have their own cap.)

East and South Asian immigrants soon followed. And immigrants from Mexico, the Dominican Republic, and other countries from which temporary workers had come during the reign of the quotas now had established lives in this country. Their presence and experience working and living in the United States created social-capital networks that were critical to facilitating future generations of immigrants' safe and productive transition to living and working here. These networks were conduits for people to come to the United States, with and without visas.

By the end of the 1970s, uneasiness was building among a few political leaders about the growing presence of undocumented immigrants. In 1969 there had been around 550,000 undocumented immigrants in the country. By 1980, just over ten years later, there would be nearly 3,000,000. Nixon's tough-on-crime rhetoric and policies collided with the campaign to paint undocumented immigrants as criminals, inaugurating a fear of immigrant crime that persists, despite not being grounded in any data on crime rates among actual immigrants.

The public responded, turning its attention to undocumented immigration in the early 1980s. Two lightning-rod events—the Mariel boat crisis, during which Americans came to believe that Fidel Castro was shipping convicts and mentally ill persons to Florida, and the drowning death of thirty Haitians trying to come to the United States on a raft—brought undocumented immigration into focus for Americans in a way that statistics alone could not. Cubans had special status due to the United States' Cold War rivalry with Communist regimes.

Haitian people, on the other hand, were treated wholly as a threat that needed to be fended off. Not only was the United States invested in propping up Haiti's vicious ruling family, the Duvaliers, but Haitian immigrants were unambiguously nonwhite. Definitions of whiteness in the United States had shifted radically enough since the 1920s that Italians and Irish had come to be considered white. But black people—US born or immigrants—have never benefited from a similar relaxing of the country's racial hierarchies.

In 1981, in response to these two events, Cubans and Haitians who arrived under irregular circumstances were made subject to mandatory detention. This was a turning point in more ways than one. Hard as it is to believe, the massive incarceration complex that now imprisons hundreds of thousands of immigrants and gobbles up billions of budget dollars did not exist at the time. Despite the periodic occurrence of raids and deportation drives throughout the late–nineteenth and twentieth centuries, mass mandatory detention represented a departure in US immigration enforcement practices. This innovation was initially propelled by the successful association of non-European immigrants with drug-related crime. Imagery intimating that black and brown immigrants were likely involved in drug crimes abounded at the time. As César Cuauhtémoc García Hernández wrote in the *UCLA Law Review:*

> It was no coincidence . . . Haitians and Cubans, the two groups against whom mandatory detention was initiated, were linked in the public imagination to crime and illegality. No more

vivid example of this popular association exists than the 1983 Hollywood blockbuster *Scarface* starring Al Pacino as a Cuban "marielito" [one who arrived on the Mariel boat lift] who becomes a top drug trafficker with an affinity for violence. This perception turned into a concern "that immigrant criminal involvement was rampant and posed a significant threat to the public's well-being," a threat represented especially poignantly by drug activity.[1]

The immigrant criminality narrative was soon joined by a second negative portrayal of immigrants that painted newcomers as likely to abuse and overtax social-rights provisions in the United States. This crystallized as the Supreme Court ruling Plyler v. Doe (1982), which clarified that immigration status cannot be a justification for refusing children the chance to go to public schools. It also extended to children of undocumented immigrants born in the United States the protections of the Fourteenth Amendment. Immigrants and their children had rights, even when they lacked proper documentation. To some, the confluence of suspected immigrant criminality and a sense that undocumented immigrants might have access to select constitutional rights did not sit well. Undocumented immigration began to capture public attention in all the wrong kinds of ways.

In response, the federal government started to focus on raids and roundups in locations where they thought undocumented immigrants would be likely to live, work, and socialize. Homes, bus stops, clubs, farms, and warehouses became sites for federal enforcement, leaving the immigrant communities around them in a state of panic.[2] As pop culture did with drug-related crime, it also portrayed fictionalized versions of the raids—for example, in the movie *Born in East L.A.*—for all to see and ponder.

As had been the case in the early 1900s, interest groups, often representing and represented by elites, were able to capitalize on this nascent anxiety about immigration and immigrants to advance their own agendas. Many of the groups were quite new at the time, but several grew in prominence throughout the 1980s and 1990s and remain powerful influences on public opinion and immigration policy to this day. Because penalties didn't yet exist for employing undocumented workers, immigration raids were often the only leverage the government had in a context where there was very little to gain by disrupting the lives of undocumented workers and their families. Indeed, when farms and workplaces were raided, employers struggled to get their crops in order and staff their businesses.

—•—

BEGINNING IN THE late 1970s, white supremacists found renewed strength in new organizations that advanced their views in tandem with other issues, including population control, antiwelfare advocacy, drug smuggling, "vice-squad" issues similar to those advocated by early border patrol advocates, and national security. In some cases, the new organizations drew on the strength of existing groups such as the Ku Klux Klan,

Aryan Nation, and other famously racist groups. The Klan announced plans to form its own militia to patrol the border looking for unauthorized crossers.[3] One figure, John Tanton, linked many of these causes and organizations. He remained a powerful force in anti-immigrant politics throughout his life, until his death in 2019.[4]

Tanton had a successful career as an ophthalmologist before his concern about the impact of overpopulation on the environment drove him into political advocacy. He tacked between superficially neutral endorsements of causes, like slowing population growth, and long-term mutually supportive affiliations with avowed white nationalists and their organizations. Some of the most important of these groups were his own creation.

Tanton's interest in stanching immigration was inspired by population-control arguments popular in the 1970s, but as early as 1969 he showed an interest in eugenics, including the possibility of forced sterilization.[5] Elsewhere in his writings he made clear that his concern about population was driven by the worry that whites were becoming a minority and would no longer be able to control the government of the United States.[6] Fear of uncontrolled population growth was embraced by environmental organizations such as Sierra Club and also gave rise to single-interest groups such as Zero Population Growth. Tanton was involved with both organizations, but neither satisfied his interest in stanching the flow of immigration into this country.

In 1979, refugees from Vietnam were targeted by a KKK campaign ostensibly agitating against a Communist presence in the United States. Tanton, apparently observing the synergy between white supremacy and a more mainstream cause, was presented with an opportunity.[7] He received financial help from a small organization that had an interest in eugenics and backing from the Scaife family, and in particular Cordelia Scaife May, heir to an enormous Mellon family fortune. May and her family were well known for ultraconservative activism, having backed the KKK's anti-Communist, anti-Vietnamese-immigrant campaign. With her support, Tanton set out to build a movement to counter what he saw as very well entrenched pro-immigration forces.

In the years since, Tanton and his colleagues received Scaife support to the tune of at least $70 million and built an empire of anti-immigrant organizations that have borne an outsized influence in shaping both public policy and public opinion. The first organization Tanton founded, the Federation for American Immigration Reform (FAIR), remains one of the most powerful anti-immigrant groups in the United States. Its mission is to push for legislative change that would severely curtail immigration. FAIR works in tandem with Tanton's second organization, the Center for Immigration Studies (CIS), which gathers and publishes data and reports casting immigration in a negative light. FAIR uses CIS-generated information in its pursuit of nativist legislative strategies. For decades, CIS has devoted itself to the agenda of FAIR, often using data that are presented as if they are objective social science but are actually cherry-picked and presented in ways that prioritize nativist propaganda rather than fact. CIS has repeatedly shown itself willing to present misleading information in the service of its agenda.[8] The third major nativist, anti-immigrant organization Tanton founded is NumbersUSA.

CIS and FAIR have been classified as hate groups by the Southern Poverty Law Center (SPLC).[9] They each employ sophisticated-seeming techniques to cloak what is often junk science. They use the language and appearance of legitimate policy and research in the service of a coordinated, decades-long attack on immigration and, crucially, on immigrants themselves. In this sense, the nativist organizations of the twenty-first century understand exactly what their predecessors in the early twentieth century did: racism presented as respectable science is a potent policy weapon.

Although Tanton accrued a long history of overtly racist, nativist, and white nationalist rhetoric, early in his activist career his political strategy largely revolved around overpopulation hysteria,[10] especially paranoia over data that dramatically compared declining fertility rates in the United States with high fertility rates throughout Latin America.[11] Tanton was fond of saying, "Demography is destiny" and wrote, "Those with their pants up are going to get caught by those with their pants down!" But Tanton's public approach quickly embraced issues related to cultural assimilation, leading him to found the group Pro-English (formerly English Language Advocates), which has promoted ballot measures and litigation aimed at banning bilingual education, requiring English fluency, and similar actions.[12]

In contemporary terms, what the racist anti-immigration activists did in the period before the mid-1990s might be termed "greenwashing": cloaking one set of motives in the language of environmental concern. Sierra Club (and other, lesser-known environmental groups) remained an important ally for Tanton through the mid-1990s, when CIS and the Sierra Club copublished *How Many Americans? Population, Immigration, and the Environment,* by Leon Bouvier and Lindsey Grant.[13] The book advocated the legal procedures that have led to mass deportations in the United States, in particular a form of deportation that deprives immigrants of due process, now known as "expedited removal." It also recommended outlawing almost all new immigration. Rarely is it reported as having been copublished. Reviews in mainstream venues treated it as the work of environmentalist population-studies scholars. And its authors had an impressive air of legitimacy; Bouvier was a demographer at Tulane and Grant a staff member at the National Security Council. Both shared a long history of advocating for low immigration and low population growth in language that avoids reference to race. But the racialized aspects of Bouvier's motivations are made visible in other venues. He published extensively with Tanton's Social Contract Press, which the Southern Poverty Law Center classifies as a hate organization and which has published openly racist texts. In one instance, Bouvier decried what he saw as a likely overtaking of European countries by Arab people.[14] He also helped introduce the language of invasion to discussions of immigration.[15]

For Tanton, partnership with liberal environmental groups remained part of a larger insidious arsenal that could woo and persuade people who weren't already inclined toward nativism and white nationalism. In a set of documents he authored known as the WITAN memos, he stated, "The issues we're touching on here must be broached by liberals. The conservatives simply cannot do it without tainting the whole subject."[16] These liberal groups enjoyed valuable forms of legitimacy that came from affiliations with professors, scientists, and other highly credentialed, respectable leaders. Keeping up the appearance of a non-nativist agenda was still important for the validity of these ventures. As the first executive director of FAIR described, they wanted to be seen as distinct from the "rednecks."[17] Little had changed since the early 1900s, when the Harvard men of the American Protective Association commissioned the nativist Dillingham report, or the 1930s, when Washington bureaucrats put a polished face on the drunken, abusive men who were drafted into the Border Patrol from the Texas Rangers.

But Tanton's superficially neutral anti-immigration advocacy cleared the way for anti-immigrant organizations that made no attempt to disguise their white nationalism. The White Citizens' Councils and its 1985 reincarnation, Council of Conservative Citizens (CCC),[18] exercised significant influence over lawmakers.[19] Like the interest groups of the early twentieth-century white nationalists, CCC was a patrician organization. Thurgood Marshall once referred to the White Citizens' Councils as "the uptown Klan." The CCC's public positions included "denigrat[ing] blacks as 'genetically inferior,' complain[ing] about 'Jewish power brokers,' calling LGBT people 'perverted sodomites,' [and] accus[ing] immigrants of turning America into a 'slimy brown mass of glop.'"[20] Unlike that of Tanton and his affiliates, CCC's interest began and ended with preventing social and cultural integration, more colloquially called "race mixing," which they believed would hasten the decline of white civilization. The CCC's statement of principles proclaimed, "We believe that the United States derives from and is an integral part of European civilization and the European people. . . . We also oppose all efforts to mix the races of mankind, to promote non-white races over the European-American people . . . , to destroy or denigrate the European-American heritage, including the heritage of the Southern people, and to force the integration of the races."[21]

Like Tanton's organizations, and facilitated by their well-connected leadership, CCC cultivated close ties to lawmakers.[22] For example, although they would both later renounce the organization, Congressman Bob Barr gave the CCC keynote speech in 1998, and then–Senate majority leader Trent Lott spoke to the group five times in the 1980s and 1990s. In some Southern states' assemblies, the CCC boasted dozens of members among the elected officials. John Tanton was a close collaborator with the so-called philosopher-king of the radical Right, CCC communications staff member Sam Francis, until Francis's death in 2005.[23] Together, Tanton and Francis launched several projects aimed at fomenting anti-immigrant sentiment, such as the fear-mongering fifty-one-episode TV show *Borderline*,[24] much of which revolved around the claim that immigrants were destroying American culture. Originally aired on the niche network NET, which was run by the far-right, antigay activist Paul Weyrich,[25] many of the episodes have now been uploaded to YouTube, where collectively they have garnered millions of views.

Ultimately, the web of nativist leaders and organizations that developed in the 1990s came to include a surprising number of names, organizations, and accomplishments, almost all of which were connected through Tanton and his groups. Richard Lamm, three-time governor of Colorado and collaborator with FAIR since its inception, wrote for CIS of the need to make immigration policy that prioritized immigrants who were culturally and linguistically likely to assimilate.[26] Garrett Hardin, an ecologist at the University of California, Santa Barbara, sought to openly foment fear that immigration from Mexico and Latin America was going to destroy the country and human civilization.[27] Peter Brimelow, founder of VDARE, a "racial realist" website,[28] has repeatedly expressed hatred for Hispanic immigrants, describing them as "special[izing] in rape, particularly of children" and making many other equally inflammatory statements.[29] In his book *Alien Nation,* Brimelow referred to immigration as causing the "browning of America."[30] Samuel Huntington, professor of political science at Harvard, capped one of the most storied academic careers of the twentieth century by publishing a lengthy book extolling the United States as a settler nation founded by Anglo-Protestants, whose qualities and commitments were uniquely capable of supporting the liberal egalitarian ethos that Hispanic immigrants were destroying.[31] In 2017, former FAIR executive director Julie Kirchner was named an advisor to the acting commissioner of CBP.[32] In fact, numerous Trump advisors and prominent members of the Trump administration have FAIR and CIS connections, including former attorney general Jeff Sessions, Advisory Commission on Election Integrity vice-chair Kris Kobach, senior advisor Stephen Miller, and many others. Tanton didn't directly generate all this activism and research, but he did lay the groundwork for supporters of racialized immigration policy and of a white nation to move into the open and succeed.

—•—

INTO THE MIX of toxic white nationalism and nativism that began to percolate in the 1980s dropped a commission to study undocumented immigration. A group of congressmen was determined to act on growing concern about the issue, in ways that would ultimately be seen as a stark betrayal of nativist causes. In 1986, after years of wrangling, Congress passed a bill that was intended to remove incentives for undocumented workers to come to the United States and to find a humane solution for the millions that had already arrived. The Immigration Reform and Control Act (IRCA) made it illegal for employers to hire undocumented workers by imposing fines on anyone caught employing an undocumented worker. The bill's more famous provision, often referred to as "amnesty," offered a one-time pathway to legal status for a select group of both legal temporary workers and undocumented workers who could document that they had lived and worked in the country for many years. Ultimately, approximately three million people regularized under IRCA. The amnesty was kind of like registry, but it targeted only people who had arrived between 1982 and 1986.

The downsides to the 1986 amnesty receive very little attention, but they have been highly consequential. The nearly sixty-year-old registry system that had been established in 1929 took a hit after 1986, when Congress passed IRCA. IRCA was meant to be a final fix to the problem of undocumented immigration, and a more efficient one than registry, which required a very long wait prior to regularization. While IRCA was being hammered out by Congress, an update to the registry date was also considered. Ultimately, Congress did move the date for registry to January 1, 1972, permitting regularization for anyone who had arrived by that date without proper documentation but who otherwise showed evidence of good moral character, generally via the absence of a criminal record. (Drug crimes and smuggling were of particular concern.) Despite the apparent redundancy with the goals of IRCA, this update was relatively uncontroversial. Generally speaking, with one exception described below, the advancement of the registry date to 1972 was supported by all lawmakers. It isn't surprising that supporters of IRCA were in favor of registry, as each bill had the same effect: regularizing people who were long-term residents in good standing. It is more surprising that opponents of amnesty supported updating registry, but in fact every member of Congress who spoke against IRCA's amnesty provisions also urged advancement of the registry date. The reason that anti-immigrant lawmakers gave for supporting registry had to do with their objections to the idea of a group amnesty such as the one embedded in IRCA. A one-time group amnesty was seen as new, potentially risky, or at least untested, and lacking the slow, gradual qualities of registry. One congressman stated:

> I oppose the very concept of such a mass amnesty, but I do believe there is a more reasonable alternative. The registry date provision approved by the Judiciary Committee would simply update an existing section of our immigration laws. . . . The registry date provision . . . is a tested and proven procedure, one that the INS is thoroughly familiar with, and I believe it is the fairest approach in dealing with the undocumented-illegal-alien problem.[33]

Another opponent of IRCA reiterated the importance of avoiding the breakup of mixed-status families, in which some members were undocumented and some were US citizens:

> There are five reasons why I think amnesty, generally, is wrong. You have an opportunity to take care of that by voting for the McCollum amendment which strikes general amnesty provisions and, in its place, leaves a provision that is in the bill called registry. Registry is a provision that allows case-by-case amnesty. It allows anybody here prior to 1976 [sic] to come forward to indicate they are married, that they have kids, that they go to school, they work, they are law abiding, they have

not been in trouble, and they can become permanent residents and then become citizens. That is fair, and I think that is compassionate. So, there is an amnesty section in the bill that survives if McCollum is successful.[34]

A few opposed the amnesty by associating it with an amorphous threat from a large wave of very recent immigrants, most of whom had arrived to do agricultural work and had lacked adequate time to become well incorporated. Characterizing very recent arrivals as an invading horde of poorly educated potential malingerers was a tactic that had been used in the 1920s. To this way of thinking, the fact that undocumented migration had increased and large numbers of people were entering the country meant that those who entered were less desirable. But these arguments were in the minority.

The one exception amid otherwise remarkable support for registry came from the attorney general, William French Smith, who spoke on behalf of the Reagan administration. Smith gave testimony counseling against advancing the registry date. Notably, he advocated for the amnesty program because "we must deal realistically with the aliens who now live in the United States illegally," "failure to act realistically merely allows the problem to grow," and "it would not be realistic to attempt widespread deportation or to allow the status quo to continue perpetuating a class of society beyond the protections and sanctions of the law." He called the amnesty program "sensible and humane." However, he described the registry date advancement as "in essence . . . set[ting] up an alternate legalization program . . . [which] would have different standards."[35] He seemed concerned that those availing themselves of the registry date could access federal benefits more quickly than immigrants trying to enter through legal means, though in practice this was a near logistical impossibility.

In many ways, IRCA established the perfect conditions for the backlash we live with today. As a practical matter, the legislation failed to put much muscle behind the provision forbidding employment of undocumented workers. After the act's passage, there was a spike in the use of familiar purging techniques such as workplace raids, but zeal for purges tends to wax and wane, and after the initial enthusiasm passed, employers who had relied on undocumented-immigrant labor carried on much as they had before. This in turn led others to enter the country undocumented, knowing that work would be available despite the new law.

Within a few years of IRCA's passage, it became clear that undocumented immigration was continuing apace, making it easy for political activists on the Right to argue that the legislation's only impact was to "reward law-breaking" through the amnesty provision. They also complained that IRCA's lack of enforcement provisions absolved or ignored the US employers that still hired undocumented workers, essentially making the federal government complicit in their practices. Indeed, opponents of immigration still accuse this decades-ago, defunct program of "incentivizing" today's undocumented immigration. This argument ignored two important facts: Registry had always been available as a means for long-term residents who didn't have legal status to become legal, and the 1986 amnesty provision applied only to a group of immigrants who came to the United States before 1983. It was quite circumscribed. In truth, after 1986 we no longer had a system in place by which an undocumented person who had lived in this country for a very long time could use that residency as a means to demonstrate eligibility for legal permanent residence.

The regularization provisions of IRCA were radicalizing to members of nativist and white nationalist groups, some of whom believed they could no longer trust the government to act on immigration issues. The provisions gave nativists an opportunity to target parts of the 1965 INA that had eliminated race quotas in immigration law. In particular, they set their sights on stigmatizing and ending family reunification. CIS and its allies argued that the amnesty was problematic because newly regularized permanent residents and citizens were allowed to sponsor visas for their close relatives. Family members came to join their foreign-born, US-citizen parents, spouses, and siblings who had regularized their status through amnesty.[36] Although the term *chain migration* had not yet been adopted by nativists, CIS's claims at the time are the same arguments that nativist opponents of family reunification use today.

The amnesty also sparked further focus on the purported fiscal liability that immigrants imposed on the United States. CIS and its friends now pivoted from emphasizing the fiscal burden of illegal immigrants to making a broader critique that immigrants of any legal status are, and will always be, low-earning, low-taxpaying, and high-public-service-using populations.[37] By the early 1990s, it became a major and enduring goal of CIS and other anti-immigrant organizations to persuade American citizens and lawmakers that immigrants are an economic drag and a financial burden on the country.

Armed with Reagan-era tactics that had already stigmatized a subset of social welfare programs aimed at the very poor, Tanton, FAIR, and CIS set about producing data designed to show that immigrants were chronic overusers of social-safety-net services. This was a challenge, in part because immigrants are unable to access a full array of US social welfare programs and in part because, over time, immigrants do not exhibit higher levels of need or usage than native-born Americans. Those holding nonimmigrant visas are generally ineligible for welfare benefits.[38] Generally, Legal Permanent Residents (LPRs) must wait five years before qualifying for federal means-tested welfare benefits, although select states provide those benefits somewhat earlier, using state tax revenues.[39] Undocumented persons are ineligible for federal entitlement and means-tested welfare programs (except for certain emergency medical care). But even leaving eligibility aside, immigrants simply are not disproportionately heavy users of social welfare. A recent Cato Institute policy brief summarizes the data:

> Overall, immigrants are less likely to consume welfare benefits and, when they do, they generally consume a lower dollar value of benefits than native-born Americans. Immigrants who meet the eligibility thresholds of age for the entitlement programs or

poverty for the means-tested welfare programs generally have lower use rates and consume a lower dollar value relative to native-born Americans. The per capita cost of providing welfare to immigrants is substantially less than the per capita cost of providing welfare to native-born Americans.[40]

Tanton, FAIR, CIS, and like-minded groups were forced to rely heavily on the narrative that immigrants were a drain on state and local economies.[41] They also insinuated that the immigrants who were seeking to come to or stay in the United States lacked useful skills and came from places that made them inherently undesirable prospective citizens.

Slowly, legislative victories began to accrue. In 1990, the United States started its first meaningful construction on a border wall, which served to reinforce both the sense that immigrants are undesirable—even lesser—people, and the unsupported belief that muscular immigration enforcement is the same thing as effective immigration laws. Border fence construction began in earnest near San Diego, and by 1993 the Border Patrol had completed a fourteen-mile stretch of fence extending inland from the Pacific Ocean.[42]

As we saw in Chapter 1, border wall construction didn't happen right away, and it remains controversial to this day. It also failed to slow the growth of the undocumented population, which steadily rose throughout the 1990s, along with authorized immigration. But a new, more focused nativist mindset was taking hold—the mindset that activists like John Tanton had been advancing at every opportunity since the late 1980s.

As was the case with the radicalizing of nativism after the IRCA amnesty, sometimes even failure worked to the benefit of anti-immigrant activism in the 1990s. Such was the case with the infamous California Proposition 187. This 1994 ballot initiative sought to prohibit undocumented immigrants from using public education, nonemergency state-provided health care, and other state services. It also attempted to mandate that public employees—including teachers, physicians, and others—report anyone who they suspected lacked legal status.[43] These were policy proposals that the Supreme Court had already stated were unconstitutional in the *Plyler* case, and though Proposition 187 was approved by voters by a margin of 59 to 41 percent, it was found unconstitutional by a federal district court and prevented from going into effect. But in the process, the public absorbed a flood of negative messages stating or implying that undocumented immigrants were soaking up precious public resources.

Nativists succeeded in deploying the Prop 187 campaign to falsely stigmatize immigrants for using social services. But because they were commited to a vision of a white America, they also exploited opportunities to stoke distrust of immigrants based on race. A new avenue for stoking racialized nativism had already been presented one year prior.[44] On February 26, 1993, a truck loaded with bombs was driven into the basement of the World Trade Center towers in New York City and detonated. This event, perpetrated by four foreign-born conspirators, sensitized the American public to the possibility of threat coming from the Middle East. Seizing an opportunity to capitalize on public anxieties, Tanton and other professional activists who had previously and publicly opposed immigration tried to draw a link between immigrants, crime, and terrorism. Groups like CIS used the terrorist attacks to highlight specific purported defects in the immigration regime and urge more restrictive reforms. For example, CIS collected detailed information—updated through 2005—on the immigration histories of active or suspected terrorists, which includes data about the World Trade Center 1993 attack and also about later attacks.[45] CIS used the fact that Ramzi Yousef, one of the perpetrators of the 1993 attacks, was not detained when he entered the country as a way to stoke fears that inadequate INS detention space was putting the country at risk for future terrorist attacks. (Yousef had asked for asylum when he entered and could have been detained.)[46] CIS also drew attention to provisions in the 1986 amnesty law that several collaborators had taken advantage of.

These arguments manipulated very understandable human fears of violence, but race and foreignness were never far from the picture. For this reason, the arguments were deeply dishonest. There has never been any evidence that foreign-born persons commit violent crimes of any variety at higher rates than native-born Americans. It is especially unlikely that a US citizen will die in a terrorist attack executed by a foreign-born person. The chance that a US citizen would be killed by a terrorist attack committed by a foreigner over a forty-year period that includes both attacks on the World Trade Center was 1 in 3.6 million.[47] But the nativist campaign to link immigration, terrorism, and crime took firm root in the American mind. This has been one of the dark successes of the elite-driven crusade to turn the American public against immigrants and immigration.

This shift was not limited to public opinion. In 1994 President Clinton directed the US Border Patrol to begin Operation Gatekeeper, designed to focus on areas of the border where many immigrants crossed. This program, and several that followed (most recently, Trump's Hold the Line), were intended to deter unauthorized crossings by forcing people to pass through dangerous areas of the desert. Operation Gatekeeper alone is responsible for approximately seven thousand deaths. Such methods, which still exist in the US immigration enforcement arsenal, essentially outsource anti-immigrant violence to criminal traffickers and to the natural forces that make deserts deadly.[48]

Through these tactics, the openness to immigration that had been inaugurated in 1965 was being replaced with a political mood that linked immigration with the two threats that Tanton and his colleagues had most successfully planted in the minds of Americans: crime and resource usage. In 1996, Congress translated this state of affairs into a set of policies and laws.

—·—

THE YEAR 1996 was a moment in US history marked by many forms of reaction and retrenchment. One of the most famous achievements of the 104th Congress was to "end welfare as we know it," replacing the long-standing social safety net with a program called Temporary Assistance for Needy Families

(TANF) and placing work requirements on parents seeking social support for their families. The Personal Responsibility and Work Opportunity Reconciliation Act (PRWORA) also made immigrants ineligible for most forms of public assistance and eliminated funds that had been available to help undocumented immigrants get legal representation.[49]

But Congress, with the support of President Clinton, enacted far more seismic changes for immigrants and immigration enforcement in a pair of bills that took direct aim at the noncitizen population of the United States. The content of these bills reflects the success that nativist activists had achieved in embedding in people's minds an entirely spurious connection between immigration and criminality. The Anti-Terrorism and Effective Death Penalty Act (AEDPA), passed in April 1996, was spurred by the 1995 terrorist attack in Oklahoma City. At the time, many sought to pin the attack on Islamic extremists, though it was actually planned and executed by two white nationalists. This had no bearing on the anti-immigration legislation process, though; AEDPA subjected any noncitizen convicted of a crime classified as an "aggravated felony" to immediate reincarceration after they finished their initial sentence.

In April of 1996 an aggravated felony was a relatively obscure and circumscribed type of crime; the category had been created in the Anti–Drug Abuse Act (ADAA) of 1988. At their origin, felonies are supposed to identify very serious crimes, usually violent ones, and have a minimum five-year penalty. ADAA had created an exception to this as part of the war on drugs—aggravated felonies require only one-year minimum sentences—but it applied narrowly to murder and to drug and gun trafficking. AEDPA added a set of very minor drug crimes to that list and diluted the severity requirement for some other crimes. It also made detention mandatory for anyone who might be subject to deportation as a result of an aggravated felony—even if their crime was so minor that they had never actually served time for it. The two bills together created a trap for immigrants in the United States. But it would take one more bill to truly weaponize AEDPA.

Five months after President Clinton signed AEDPA into law, in September of 1996, Congress passed the Illegal Immigration Reform and Immigrant Responsibility Act (IIRIRA) with the support of the White House. The bill had several parts, some of which applied to legal residents and others of which addressed undocumented immigrants. Working in tandem with AEDPA, the bill vastly expanded the number and type of crimes for which a legal resident of the United States could be deported. AEDPA had made aggravated felonies, some of which came with one-year sentences, a trigger for mandatory incarceration of immigrants after serving their sentences. But even after the AEDPA expansion, there weren't many crimes classified as aggravated felonies. IIRIRA exploded those boundaries, adding a long list of minor crimes—classified for citizens as misdemeanors—to the category. Examples of crimes that IIRIRA reclassified as aggravated felonies include gambling, document fraud, forgery, bribery, counterfeiting, skipping bail, failing to appear in court, obstruction of justice, perjury, and all controlled-substance offenses. People have wound up in deportation proceedings for no more than patting a family member on the backside or possession of 2.5 grams of marijuana.[50] One immigration judge expressed a widely held view, saying, "Non-violent, fairly trivial misdemeanors are considered aggravated felonies under our immigration laws."[51]

If you're a skeptical person and you're thinking to yourself that there's no reason to tolerate the presence of someone who committed even a minor misdemeanor, especially if they are undocumented, consider this: The law mandates that anyone— even a minor—can be declared inadmissible and permanently barred from a pathway to lawful permanent residence if there is a "reason to believe" that they committed a crime. This is even true if they have been tried before a jury and found innocent.[52]

The reclassification of misdemeanors into aggravated felonies also meant that noncitizens could be deported without even a hearing in front of an immigration judge.[53] It precluded all judicial review of deportation orders based on criminal convictions, including via habeas corpus. Shockingly to many who believe this is not possible in the United States, the measure is retroactive. Crimes that were misdemeanors when they were committed can be reclassified for immigration purposes, making an offense that wasn't a deportation trigger when it was committed into a deportable offense going forward.[54] IIRIRA also makes it difficult for anyone who has undergone a deportation, for however trivial a reason and with scant or no due process, to legally return to the United States. "Unlawful presence bars" raise barriers to reentry that start at three years and in many cases are lifelong. Although laws exist to "cancel" removal orders in so-called hardship cases—for example, when deportation would cause extreme hardship to a spouse or child who is a US citizen—people who are deported because of an aggravated-felony conviction are ineligible for such relief.[55] Because the US government did not even try to keep reliable records on its use of the aggravated felony as a basis for deportation, we know remarkably little about who has fallen victim to these procedures and whether the procedures are being used in accordance with the law.[56] One thing that is clear is that a large proportion of people deported this way entered the United States legally and had been living in the country for a long time.[57]

The 1996 law magnified the association of immigrants with crime in other ways. The bill inserted a small provision that drafted state and local police into immigration law enforcement. This so-called 287(g) provision permitted what are known as Memoranda of Understanding, in which the attorney general can enter into agreements with state and local law enforcement to enforce immigration law. The 287(g) agreements were critical to a number of aggressive immigration enforcement programs that have proven to be ineffective and dangerous. One prominent example is Secure Communities, a program that originated in the Bush era, was phased out during Obama's presidency, and has been restarted by President Trump. Secure Communities was designed to crack down on criminal immigrants via federal, state, and local partnerships. A series of studies has shown that Secure Communities not only was ineffective at making communities safer but actually eroded law enforcement's ability to operate by discouraging anyone who was worried about being targeted from cooperating with police investigations or reporting crimes.

After 1996, immigrants who committed misdemeanors were felons, for legal purposes, and their aggravated felonies meant they were both reincarcerated after serving sentences and subject to deportation. The human consequences of this shift have been catastrophic. And the price of inflicting those consequences on immigrants and their families has been equally immense. No policy, law, or event since the creation of the Border Patrol in 1924 did as much to facilitate mass deportation or to spark out-of-control growth of the immigration enforcement bureaucracy as the two measures passed in 1996. The legal apparatus necessary to act on nativist impulses—to systematically build a whiter nation—was coming into existence, ushering in the era of mass incarceration of immigrants and mass deportation. As if these drastic shifts in rules about deportability were not enough, IIRIRA also clarified and expanded the legal basis for border wall construction.[58] The law required that a three-tiered barrier be built to reinforce the fourteen-mile stretch of fence and authorized the construction of additional barriers and roads "in the vicinity of the United States border."[59]

This legal trifecta allowed the INS to build itself a direct pipeline from the US criminal-punishment system, which was itself mushrooming throughout the 1990s, into the immigration enforcement apparatus. That pipeline has fed the precipitous growth of ICE to this day, long after undocumented immigration peaked. It is difficult to overstate how significant this call for mandatory detention has been to the growth of the nation's immigration enforcement system, in particular the detention infrastructure that soaks up so many resources.

By the mid-1990s, the long-standing campaign against immigrants and the legislative action it inspired succeeded in cementing in many people's minds a spurious connection between immigration and criminality. The tendency to associate immigration with lawlessness had been present all along—at least since Border Patrol was sent to borderland towns on vice-squad missions dreamed up by people living in other parts of the country. But by the 1990s, something had changed. In the past, harsh anti-immigration legislation had been paired with forms of amnesty. The invention of registry and its extension had been a part of the most nativist and punitive actions Congress had taken. This was not true in 1996. Neither a registry update nor any other law to adjust the status of long-term undocumented residents was enacted.

IIRIRA wasn't just important because it gave the government license to build fencing, deny immigrants social welfare resources, treat immigrants as criminals, and close avenues for immigrants' due process rights. It was important because the new laws made people believe that there were problems to solve. Never mind that walls can't keep out people who enter legally, that immigrants posed no threat to citizens, or that due process exists to protect all persons, including noncitizens, and to protect the rule of law itself. News reports about deportation numbers, aggravated felonies, wall construction, and welfare usage made it hard to escape the belief that the country was under siege.

During Clinton's presidency, a succession of bills intended to accomplish an update to the registry date—one of the only ways to effectively reduce the undocumented population—was introduced in the 106th Congress, but none were enacted or even made serious progress.[60] The "deadline" date for immigrants who had entered the country without documentation to register for naturalization remained fixed at 1972. And whereas at the start of the decade 3.5 million undocumented immigrants resided in the United States, by 1999, 8.5 million did.[61]

Although the late 1990s was a period of high immigration, there were not more people entering the United States (as a proportion of the entire population) than there had been early in the century. What had changed was the invention of illegality between 1924 and 1929 and the elimination of any means for long-term residents to adjust their status.

Immigrant rights advocates saw that 1996 brought a sea change for undocumented immigrants. It wasn't yet clear, though, that this would cost US citizens as dearly as we now know it did. Mass deportation was a possibility, but DHS, ICE, and CBP did not yet exist. The country didn't spend enough money or have enough infrastructure in place to do the kinds of things we read about in Chapter 1. Citizens had every reason to feel safe, even if immigrants felt the chill in the air. But things were about to change.

CHAPTER SEVEN

Nervous Breakdown

By 2001, THE UNITED STATES HAD BEEN PRIMED FOR THE KIND OF war on immigrants that nativists and white nationalists had been preparing to wage for well over a decade. The country was still experiencing high levels of immigration, and in the absence of any means for undocumented people to adjust their status, their numbers grew each year. Many had been in the country for quite a while and had spouses and children who were US citizens.

On September 11 of that year, a coordinated set of terror attacks was launched by Al Qaeda operatives, who hijacked four planes. The Twin Towers of New York City's World Trade Center and the Pentagon were successfully targeted. A fourth target was spared after passengers thwarted hijackers, leading to the fatal crash of their plane in a Pennsylvania field. The event remains the single deadliest terrorist attack in US history. It shook the nation and the world and sent the United States into wars that have now lasted almost two decades. And it created an opportunity for nativists to mobilize all the fears about immigrants they had been fomenting in support of an enormous enforcement buildup that contributed nothing to national security or public safety.

—•—

EVEN THOUGH CONGRESS and activist organizations had put in place a very sturdy anti-immigrant framework in the 1990s, before 9/11 the American public remained cautiously optimistic and supportive regarding both immigration and immigrants. In a 2000 Gallup poll, 54 percent of respondents said that immigration levels should be kept the same or increased.[1] To understand what sent immigration enforcement off the rails in spite of the widespread support for immigrants, one must return to the immediate political aftermath of the 9/11 terrorist attacks and trace how reactions to those attacks were exploited in the service of nativism, to the detriment of national security.

Even before the identities of the attackers were confirmed, while the Twin Towers were still smoldering, nativists saw an opportunity to advance their agenda. The country was anxious and suspicious, deeply fearful that other attackers were lurking inside the United States and abroad. While Congress began discussing the creation of the Department of Homeland Security, organizations working in the Tanton mold sprang into action to exploit those fears. In 2002, CIS released a study titled "The Open Door: How Militant Islamic Terrorists Entered and Remained in the United States, 1993–2001."[2] This study—along with dozens of other stories CIS ran about 9/11 in the ensuing decade—sought to underscore in people's minds a spurious connection between immigration and national security.[3] CIS examined aspects of the immigration system that conceivably contributed to the 9/11 hijackers' ability to enter the country and gestured at others that they imagined could enable the entry of a future, hypothetical attacker.[4] Their reports and stories focused on lax screening of people who obtained particular immigrant statuses, the supposed ease of "absconding to" or "disappearing into" the United States, and visa overstays. In one study, CIS claimed that fraudulent marriage-based green card applications were "prevalent among international terrorists, including members of Al-Qaeda."[5]

As Tanton and his network continued their drumbeat of restriction, other nativists began to organize around these issues. The anti-immigrant group Americans for Legal Immigration PAC (ALIPAC) formed on September 11, 2004, "in honor of the victims of 9/11."[6] ALIPAC's goal is to "stop and reverse illegal immigration."[7] ALIPAC has funded candidates for the anti-immigrant Tea Party and it continued to invoke the memory of 9/11 in its political activity long after it was clear that the organization's goals were not substantively connected to terrorist attacks. For example, in an email sent out on September 11, 2013, ALIPAC led with the subject line "Illegals are hijacking our government: Let's roll Americans."[8] Their message was one of unvarnished nativism.

At the same time, Congress and President George W. Bush undertook a hasty but sweeping response to the 9/11 attacks. Ultimately this response yielded one of the most massive reorganizations of the US government in the modern era. It was initiated ostensibly to prevent future terrorist attacks. Eleven days after the attack, President Bush announced that he would create an Office of Homeland Security (OHS) in the White House, which he did via Executive Order 13228 on October 8, 2001. He described the goal: "The mission of the Office [of Homeland Security] shall be to develop and coordinate the implementation of a comprehensive national strategy to secure the United States from terrorist threats or attacks."[9] Bush hoped to maintain Homeland Security as an executive-branch office subject to exclusive presidential control, and he opposed the creation of a cabinet-level department. But once congressional action appeared likely, the president assembled a team to draft a legislative proposal, and in June 2002 he formally submitted a proposal to Congress.[10] The Homeland Security Act, signed into law in November 2002, united functions and departments related to border and transportation security into the new Department of Homeland Security (DHS). The department's overarching role was to focus on preventing terrorists and explosives from entering the country, emergency preparedness, countermeasures against mass weapons, information analysis, and infrastructure protection.[11]

The creation of DHS is considered the largest reorganization of the federal government since the Department of Defense was created in 1947. For such a sweeping reform, it was not a popular bill and passed by only one vote. But bills that pass by one vote are enacted just the same as those with strong support. This bill dramatically altered the course of our country's history.[12]

Although the stated need for a new cabinet-level department was to enhance national security in light of terrorist threats, the most profound of its consequences by far has been to direct an unprecedented amount of resources to fund and empower activities that are entirely unrelated to national security. As we saw in the first two chapters, these billions pay for indiscriminate mass deportation as well as the dangerous activities that accompany an unchecked immigration apparatus. Quite a bit of this money ultimately ends up in the hands of private businesses whose main work is self-enrichment and the enforcement of a nativist, anti-immigrant agenda.

The reorganization triggered by the creation of DHS disassembled the Immigration and Naturalization Service (INS) that had been operative since 1933 and divided its activities among three agencies: United States Citizenship and Immigration Services (USCIS), CBP, and ICE.[13] In 2010, an additional step was taken when ICE subdivided itself, creating separate divisions for enforcement and removals: Enforcement and Removal Operations (ERO) and Homeland Security Investigations (HSI).[14] Each juncture at which immigration-related responsibilities were divided among more specialized subunits has contributed to an overall trend in which enforcement activities—hunting for undocumented immigrants, incarcerating them, and deporting them—have skyrocketed, while other extremely important activities like ensuring due process, courtroom justice, and even the processing of naturalization applications[15] have been starved. Most notably absent from ICE and CBP's priorities are activities related to homeland security.

Astronomical budgets and agency structures that funnel money away from national security and toward anti-immigrant hysterics are made possible by the uniquely malleable mission of DHS and the incredibly wide and specialized set of agencies that fall under its authority. Whereas the function and missions of other cabinet-level agencies remain relatively if not entirely constant over decades and even centuries, DHS's mission is rearticulated each year in the "Budget Message of the President" that prefaces the formal government budget. A review of the presidents' budget messages since DHS was established offers meaningful insight into the transformation of the department's mission from one of coordinating a complicated array of security functions to one in which generic immigration control activities crowd out other priorities. The president's budget statement in 2003 offered this vision for DHS:

> The higher priority we all now attach to homeland security has already begun to ripple through the land. The Government of the United States has no more important mission than fighting terrorism overseas and securing the homeland from future terrorist attacks. . . . We will find new and im-

portant ways to encourage citizens to be more alert and active in their communities. We will succeed in weaving an effective and permanent level of security into the fabric of a better, safer, stronger America.[16]

Between 2003 and 2005, DHS's "mission" or "themes" largely focused on identifying threats in the form of cargo or high-risk persons; biodefense; securing transportation systems; and, insofar as ICE was concerned, targeted enforcement, like workplace raids in sensitive industries.[17] But by 2010 the Obama administration had settled on five very differently framed action areas: Guarding Against Terrorism; Securing Our Borders (defined as "prevent[ing] and investigat[ing] illegal movements across our borders, including the smuggling of people, drugs, cash, and weapons"); Smart and Tough Enforcement of Immigration Laws and Improving Immigration Services; Preparing for and Responding to Natural Disasters; and Unifying and Maturing DHS.[18] Through 2016, this mix remained constant, although Cybersecurity replaced the section Maturing DHS.[19]

Then, in 2017 and 2018, terrorism was again demoted in significance—it was removed from top billing for the first time since DHS's creation. Two priorities replaced preventing terrorism: Securing Our Borders ("to stop illegal migrants, criminals, and terrorists") and Enforcing our Immigration Laws (by way of generalized interior enforcement by ICE).[20] To anyone following closely since the early 1990s, this move represented the culmination of a strategy to equate the idea of a national security threat with border control and immigration, not just in the minds of white nationalists or even conservatives but in the very structure of the nation's security apparatus.

Even these quite dramatic shifts in DHS's mission statement don't reveal the degree to which DHS has been transformed from an umbrella organization established to oversee national security–related agencies into a border patrol and deportation machine. The extent to which its early mission statements are belied by the actual appropriations and activities of its subsidiary components is breathtaking. In the years since its inception, less than two decades ago, generic immigration control work—mass deportation of mostly law-abiding people with little or no connection to national security concerns—has absorbed the budgets and the attention of the security apparatus.

It is easy to see how relatively low a priority national security activities have become when we compare the responsibilities and budgets of ICE's deportation arm (ERO) and its security arm (HSI and HSI's predecessors). Early on, the money requested for immigration enforcement in the name of national security at least appeared as though it was being requested to perform security-related work. For fiscal year 2003, at least 63 percent of ICE's budget requests were for activities that, as ICE is now organized, would fall under HSI's mandate.[21] But by 2011, the first full year in which HSI existed as a separate entity, the funding ratio had switched: activities within HSI's security-related mandate received $1.92 billion in funding, whereas work within ERO's portfolio for generic immigration enforcement received far more money: $2.57 billion.[22] The disparity widens through 2017, when HSI received

$2.07 billion and ERO $3.71 billion.[23] Then the disparity becomes a crevasse. In fiscal year 2018, ICE's budget requests allocated HSI $2.02 billion to ERO's $4.86 billion, and for fiscal year 2019, ERO's budget stays at $4.86 billion while HSI's *decreases* to $1.61 billion.[24] Just fifteen years after the creation of DHS, work explicitly related to security receives only a small fraction—slightly over one-third—of the funding that goes to generic removal operations.

Even within HSI's increasingly anemic portfolio, national security is being crowded out by generic immigration enforcement. Ninety percent of HSI's budget is devoted to the parts of its work that are most closely related to deportation.[25] HSI has three distinct program areas: Domestic Investigations, International Operations, and Intelligence.[26] Domestic Investigations is tasked with locating and investigating terrorists and transnational crime or security threats, and with removing aliens *who pose a threat to national security.*[27] International Operations funds offices abroad to conduct law enforcement, combat transnational crime, and target human, narcotics, weapons, and technology trafficking. International Operations is one important venue through which the sexual exploitation of children is investigated. It also screens visa applicants from high-risk areas for potential national security and public safety concerns.[28] Finally, Intelligence works to collect and share information about illegal trade and financial activity in the United States. Intelligence also "prepares ICE for agency-wide continuity of operations, emergency response, and crisis management. Its employees gather information to identify tactics, techniques, and procedures to counter public safety and national security threats while ensuring force protection and officer safety."[29]

Despite HSI's rhetorical commitment to terrorism as a top priority, it starves its International Operations and Intelligence units in favor of data collection on visa applicants, people here on visas, visa overstays, workplaces suspected of hiring immigrants in violation of federal law, and smuggling (drugs, money, and to a lesser extent guns). In fact, the spying and collection of data on protesters in the United States that was mentioned at the very beginning of the book was originally done by HSI, despite the fact that those protests lacked any connection to threats of terrorism. Furthermore, HSI's surveillance of nonviolent protestors took attention away from thwarting attacks like the Tree of Life synagogue massacre in Pittsburgh, church burnings, and other acts of terrorism.[30] DHS even hired a private contractor to conduct additional surveillance on protestors.[31]

In contrast to security operations under HSI, ERO is flush with cash. It uses its resources for relatively indiscriminate incarceration and deportation. ERO has five projects: Custody Operations, Fugitive Operations, Criminal Alien Program (CAP), Alternatives to Detention (ATD), and Transportation and Removal Program (TRP). In 2017, Custody Operations received $2.71 billion of the total $3.71 billion ERO budget.[32] Of the $1.1 billion increase sought in 2018 for ERO's 2019 activities, $800 million is slated for Custody Operations.[33] As its name implies, Custody Operations involves taking people into custody—for example, ICE arrests in the streets, courthouses, workplaces, and homes. Since Trump issued an executive order changing immigration enforcement priorities, ICE arrests have increased by 43 percent, Notice to Appear (NTA) issuances (the first step in deporting someone) have increased by 48 percent, and ICE detainers (when local law enforcement, at the request of ICE, holds someone otherwise eligible for release) have increased by 82 percent.[34] At the same time, the average length of stay in ICE detention has increased to fifty-one days.[35] Under the Trump administration, ICE has been able to reverse past policy constraints that required the agency to focus on criminal aliens and discouraged the agency from pursuing undocumented immigrants with no criminal record.

Until recently, the enormous budgets of any one of these agencies would have been unimaginable, particularly to conservatives who have long advocated for reduced government spending. Similarly, in the years immediately following 9/11 it would have been unthinkable to announce to the public that a government agency was going to siphon huge amounts of money away from protecting the country from potential terrorist attacks in order to search for and deport undocumented immigrants who don't pose a threat to anyone. Although nativist rhetoric invokes ideas of national security all the time, the nativist agenda has deprioritized security at every turn.

The good news is that foreign-born terrorists don't appear to be lurking around each corner, as many claimed when DHS was formed. Nor is this likely to change; right now the largest group of people trying to enter the country without permission is Central American. Not a single person from that region has ever committed a terrorist act on US soil.[36] But domestic terrorism is a very real threat in the United States. It grows each year, often miscategorized and systematically neglected by a DHS that is fixated on law-abiding immigrants. While churches have burned and the country has learned to live in fear of mass shootings, ICE beats the drum of nativism inherited from 1990s white nationalists. Investigative reporting has shown very clear orders given to ICE employees to cherry-pick lurid stories of immigrant crime even when those stories do not represent the people ICE hunts for and deports; in some cases, ICE workers are being asked to substantiate outright lies on the part of Trump.[37]

That immigration enforcement budgets have ballooned since the establishment of DHS is not in question. In 2003, when DHS was instituted, the country spent around $3.3 billion annually on CBP and $6 billion on ICE, a massive increase over budgets in the 1990s, when undocumented immigration was rapidly rising.[38] Undocumented entries are now at a forty-six-year low, with the overall undocumented population shrinking. Yet in 2019 CBP requested a whopping $14.2 billion, and ICE's request had leaped to $8.8 billion. CBP received $14.96 billion and ICE received $7.59 billion, before any overspending or siphoning of resources from the army or FEMA budgets.[39]

One of the worrisome transformations that has accompanied this massive growth of enforcement spending has been the diversion of large portions of ICE's budget and responsibilities to private companies that are tasked with handling detention and monitoring. A cruel and wasteful immigration apparatus is the lifeblood of these companies, their employees, and sometimes even the towns in which their facilities are located. President Obama had committed the federal government to moving away from private prison and detention companies (for both immigration and nonimmigration functions) after an audit found that private companies were responsible for more security and safety violations than government-run facilities.[40] However, his order was rescinded during the Trump administration by US Attorney General Jeff Sessions early in his tenure.

The amount of public money that ends up in the coffers of private corporations has intentionally been made difficult to discern. DHS reports its activities by agency (e.g., ICE, CBP) and activity (e.g., detention, airline operations) rather than stating directly how much it awards in contracts to any given private firm. This obscures how much public money private companies are receiving via contracts for detention and monitoring of detainees. But there are ways to approximate these costs. For example, if we multiply the total detention expenditure ($2.97 billion in 2017[41]) by a factor of two-thirds (roughly the proportion of detention beds that is managed by private facilities), we arrive at a figure of $1.93 billion spent on private detention.

However, the Trump administration's recommitment to privatization has occurred despite the fact that private facilities most likely cost more than their public counterparts—assuming that immigrant detention spending follows the same patterns as general inmate incarceration.[42] That would make the $1.93 billion expenditure an underestimate. Searching ICE's reported expenditures company by company provides greater clarity, even though readily available data fail to capture all the private facilities that are not owned by publicly traded companies. Still, we can get a good sense of things because just a few companies—CoreCivic, the GEO Group, and BI Incorporated (acquired by GEO Group in 2011)—do the lion's share of this work. CoreCivic and GEO run eight of the country's largest immigration jails. BI Incorporated offers alternatives to detention programming for ICE, providing services such as electronic ankle monitoring. According to a congressional report,[43] CoreCivic and GEO Group together made $478 million from ICE detentions in 2014. By 2017, the amount the companies reported making had nearly doubled, to $871 million.[44] The DHS's Office of the Inspector General wrote an entire report about how one ICE contract that benefited CoreCivic (also known as CCA) violated federal procurement laws.[45] But as we have seen, ICE and CBP are not always responsive to government and internal investigations, even when they turn up physical abuses by their agents. In any event, CoreCivic revenue from ICE contracts has soared in the last few years.[46]

The companies that receive these lucrative contracts heap campaign contributions on elected officials who have special authority over the contracts. This incentivizes members of Congress to support private contracts for detention and monitoring work. The Center for Responsive Politics reports that CoreCivic's contributions to candidates running for federal office by its PACs, its employees, and outside groups increased from just $6,000 in the 1990 election cycle to roughly $249,000 in 2016.[47] The GEO Group donates even more: over $1.2 million in the 2016 cycle, up from about $139,000 in 2004. In addition to donating to campaigns, GEO has also spent heavily on lobbying Congress— from $120,000 in 2004 to $1 million in 2016. CoreCivic put $10.6 million toward immigration lobbying between 2008 and 2014; of this total, $9,760,000 was used to lobby congresspeople on the House Appropriations Committee Homeland Security Subcommittee, which sets the detention budget. These are good investments for the companies' bottom line. In August 2016, when the Justice Department announced it would not extend further contracts, the stock values of GEO Group and CoreCivic fell by 39 percent and more than 35 percent, respectively.[48] Right after Attorney General Sessions indicated that the Trump administration would rescind the Obama-era plan to wind down the use of private facilities, CoreCivic and GEO Group stocks increased by 137 percent and 98 percent, respectively.[49]

—•—

AS WE HEAD toward the 2020 election, let's take stock of what has unfolded over the course of almost exactly a hundred years. Between 1924 and 1929, Congress created the status of undocumented immigration by first banning immigration from most countries and then creating penalties for breaking those laws. The 1924 National Origins Act, the enactment of which had been a longtime goal of a set of elite actors, was motivated by animus toward the races and ethnicities represented in the immigrant pool at the time. As Congress took the final steps to impose penalties on undocumentedness, it also made sure that a system was in place for undocumented residents who had been in the country for a lengthy period to adjust their status and get on track to become citizens. From the 1930s through the early 1960s, a small, modestly resourced, and frequently corrupt and abusive Border Patrol enforced the laws enacted in the 1920s. Mass deportation was not yet possible, but the roundups that threw large numbers of people out of the country were expressions of racialized violence. They took a high toll on the individuals who were subject to them and on the communities in which they lived.

In 1965, a radical transformation of immigration law opened the nation's borders to higher levels of immigration and greater numbers of immigrants from around the world. But the people who made the law were not seeking a radical demographic transformation of the US population. They clearly thought they had crafted their legislation in a way that would forestall what ended up happening: mass immigration of people from countries that had not previously sent many immigrants to the United States. Within fifteen years, anxiety and a nascent backlash were building. At first, Congress took what now looks like a modest approach. They created penalties for employing undocumented workers but also approved a pathway to citizenship for millions of undocumented and temporary workers. Still, the tide was turning. Nativist and white nationalist activists gained traction, especially after the 1993 attack on the World Trade Center. And throughout the 1990s, Congress built legislative support for mass deportation.

That legislation would be put to use after the second attack on the World Trade Center and after the creation of DHS and the division of INS's work into three separate agencies: ICE, CBP, and USCIS. In the intervening years, the nation's immigration enforcement has morphed into an abusive, out-of-control colossus that grows more expensive, cruel, and dangerous each year.

The Abolish ICE movement had a brief moment in 2018, but most people don't take seriously the idea that we could eliminate the nation's largest federal law-enforcement agency, even though, as this book's timeline shows, that is analogous to what Congress did in 2003, when it created DHS. Of course, ICE is only part of the country's immigration enforcement apparatus, and only part of the abusive culture associated with that apparatus. Some version of CBP, an enormous agency in its own right, has been around far longer than ICE.

In the absence of any means to return the country to an era when DHS didn't exist and IIRIRA and AEDPA had not been enacted, what steps can we take to rein in the people and institutions that increasingly threaten immigrants, US citizens, and the rights that people in this country hold dear? In the Conclusion, I offer some suggestions, with an eye to how the government has acted to address immigration concerns in the past.

Conclusion
Where Do We Go from Here?

THANKSGIVING WEEK OF 2018, WHEN I FINISHED AN EARLY draft of this book, was a festive time for most Americans, but it was no holiday for immigration enforcement or for the desperate immigrants they were ordered to pursue. Cable news shows ran hours of coverage showing US troops at the southern border unrolling razor wire in what had become a theater of war against Central American asylum seekers heading toward the United States. President Trump had authorized troops to use lethal force, if need be, to hold them off at the border. Meanwhile, on Twitter, an immigration lawyer described asking a judge if his client could be excused from the courtroom because she was being fussy, whimpering, and crying. His client was a two-year-old girl alone at her deportation hearing, and she was hardly the only toddler who has been dragged into court by the US government. At the time, HHS was holding fourteen thousand other children in detention facilities. Some of those facilities were just tents in the desert—lucrative operations for the private companies who had government contracts with ICE, but not nearly adequate to meet even the most basic needs of terrified, traumatized children.

Critics who clamor to "Abolish ICE" are not wrong to declare that the agency is harming immigrants and US citizens. CBP is dangerous, too, even if many have been slower to recognize that fact. And the Department of Homeland Security has sanctioned the abuses within both agencies. Furthermore, although the scope and visibility of the abuses perpetrated under DHS are pronounced, the organizations that preceded ICE and CBP engaged in the same kinds of practices, if not always with the budgets and tools to accomplish the same volume of abuse. It seems to matter little who is in charge, who is president, or even whether large numbers of undocumented immigrants are actually entering and staying in the country. These problems persist when Democrats are in office and when Republicans are in office. Politicians in thrall to the same forces of nativism and white nationalism that have influenced the citizenry have denied Americans comprehensive immigration reform. In 2013, the Senate passed a bill to reform immigration, but then-speaker John Boehner refused even to allow a floor debate in the House, partly for reasons fed to him by CIS.[1] Among the other proposals that were on the cusp of success but ultimately failed to achieve sufficient support in Congress have been several that would have put people brought to the United States without authorization when they were children (popularly called DREAMers) on a pathway to citizenship. Ultimately, President Obama oversaw the enactment of Deferred Action for Childhood Arrivals (DACA), which allowed a subset of so-called DREAMers to stay, work, and attend school in this country. However, they were denied a pathway to citizenship, and their fragile semi-citizenship has been on the chopping block since Trump came into office.

At no point in the last two decades has retrenchment of the massive immigration enforcement apparatus been on the horizon. Our "enforcement at any cost" mentality grows more firmly rooted with each passing year and every administration, at the border and in the interior, regardless of whether the people seeking entry are fleeing unsustainable economies or deadly violence. Although congressional Democrats have fought Trump on the idea of the wall, many have conceded most of the ground on funding enforcement, euphemistically referring to "border security" even though the most—possibly the only—menacing security threat at the border is CBP itself. Until Congress produces changes in how we deal with both immigration and citizenship, we cannot expect our legislators—or anyone else—to effectively rein in the agencies charged with enforcing those laws. One cannot underscore this point enough. As long as we cling to immigration and citizenship laws that prioritize the bad intentions of people who want a whiter America and the companies making money from unnecessary and harsh enforcement, that apparatus will remain a threat. And as long as the apparatus is intact, all the reliable information we have about the importance of immigration and the dangers of un-checked enforcement won't get us out of our predicament.

At least three changes need to be implemented if we want to root out the sources of the power that have enabled our im-migration enforcement agencies to run amok and deny any fu-ture agency the justification to behave as lawlessly as ICE and CBP do. By way of conclusion, I sketch the broad outline of these changes.

Possibly the most transformational step Congress could and should take does not involve laying a hand on ICE, CBP, or DHS. If one overarching lesson can be found in the history of immigration, it is that enforcement tends to fail at achieving its stated goals and also tends to backfire, leaving unintended consequences in its wake. At the root of enforcement is the legislative structure that makes some people "legal" and others "illegal." That structure is the artifact of racist and badly con-ceived laws, passed in the 1920s, for the purpose of forging a whiter nation. But for those laws, we might have much more sensible laws to legally accommodate immigrants who live in the United States for long periods of time and wish to stay, as well as those who need to come and go.

In the United States right now, over ten million people lack legal status. Two-thirds of them have been in the coun-try for more than ten years, and almost half of all the house-holds in which they live include children who were born in the United States and thus have US citizenship. These circumstances—particularly the decades-long residents who have become Americans in all senses except for their legal status—would have been abhorrent to the founders and even to congresspeople from 1929 to the 1990s, most of whom regarded lengthy residence as the sign of a committed, hopeful citizen. Even during periods when US immigration law has been formulated by unapologetically racist members of Congress, most of them have acknowledged that even irregular immigrants become citizenly after they have lived, worked, and raised families in the country for years. To them, the idea that we would refuse to recognize this fact in our citizenship laws constitutes a stain on the nation.

But as long as the most salient *legal* fact about undocumented persons is the single moment at which they entered without papers or an inspection, or overstayed a visa, ICE and CBP lack any reason to stop their lawless empire building. They may not even have a way to stop. The Iron Law of Oligarchy tells us that bureaucracies struggle to self-discipline even when their own members seek change. They must be brought into compliance by legislation that denies them not just limitless budgets and authority but also the population of subjects they use to justify their abusive and lawless behavior. Their very reason for existing must be diminished.

People's entrance and presence in a country can only be "illegal" if rules prohibit and punish their entry and presence. Despite the fact that the law recognizes that unauthorized entry is not a serious or dangerous violation, being undocumented is one of the only triggers for severe, permanent criminal penalties with no statute of limitations. Crossing the border without papers and an inspection is only a misdemeanor. Overstaying a visa is a civil violation, not a crime.

The good news is that we don't need to pass an entirely new set of laws to reduce the population of undocumented people who are currently eligible for deportation. We can take a huge step forward simply by reviving the statute of limitations on undocumentedness in the registry date and ensuring that the date is automatically updated in the future. Reinstating a statute of limitations through an update to registry would create a gradual, nondisruptive process that periodically promotes longtime undocumented residents who are otherwise law-abiding residents to legal residency, and eventually citizenship, thereby preventing the perpetual growth of the undocumented population.

Recall a few features of the history of registry. It was created in 1929, and the date was last advanced in 1986. Currently it only applies to people who arrived in the country by 1972. The lawmakers who created and updated registry were outspoken opponents of open borders. In some cases, they wanted very stringent border controls, and not always for good reasons. That merits discussion. But they uniformly recognized that individuals who live in the United States for long periods of time without committing serious crimes need and deserve the opportunity to acquire citizenship. In fact, people who live anywhere for many years, raise families, develop friendships, work, go to school, and do all the other things that we associate with "citizenliness" have, in essence, become citizens. The drafters of this country's early naturalization laws understood that democracies have a responsibility to confer political status and rights on individuals who have the attributes of citizens. Now that the undocumented population is increasingly composed of long-term residents, it is time to take that responsibility seriously.

What would this mean in practical terms? In the wake of the 1986 update to registry, there was a brief spike in the number of people who used the law to naturalize. In 1987, 8,153 used it, and by 1988 that figure topped out at 40,029.[2] The highest number since then was in 1990, when 4,651 people naturalized via registry.[3] After that, the numbers have declined, and now virtually no one can or does use registry. From the 1990s through 2007, the undocumented population in the United States rose; since then it has plateaued and declined.[4] If registry were to be gradually updated to bring it back into line with the expectations of the original legislation, the number of people who use it would most likely spike dramatically. But spikes—in both regularization and immigration itself—are temporary, and the increase would reflect the naturalization of individuals who by almost any reasonable measure are indistinguishable from citizens, aside from their legal status. And since irregular entry and the undocumented population have both been steadily shrinking for over a decade, the spike might well be short lived. Remember that as recently as 2015, roughly two-thirds of Americans surveyed supported a pathway to citizenship for undocumented immigrants who can meet some basic requirements over time.[5] Registry *is* that pathway. It doesn't require massive, complex legislation. It already exists. It just needs a deadline that gradually and periodically updates.

The many Americans who support regularization of undocumented immigrants have good instincts. When immigrants who are out of status are regularized, the US economy benefits. A National Bureau of Economic Research study that examined the consequences of legalization and citizenship on the country's GDP found that the regularization of unauthorized immigrants increases their income by 25 percent. The researchers used this information to run three different models predicting how a 2013 regularization plan would affect the US economy over a ten-year period. The most generous plan, involving immediate regularization for eligible undocumented people and providing a pathway to citizenship, projected a cumulative increase in GDP of approximately $1.4 trillion.[6] A pathway to citizenship was also predicted to increase the earnings of all Americans by $791 billion and add 203,000 jobs.[7] A more conservative plan that only allowed undocumented individuals to be regularized, without a pathway to citizenship, was projected to add about $832 billion to the US economy— not insubstantial, but far less than would regularization.

Immigrants have a positive impact on GDP, earnings, and employment for several reasons. Immigrant skill sets tend to complement those of native-born Americans. Immigration is also correlated with a decrease in the offshoring of jobs. But neither US citizens nor the country's immigrant population can maximize the mutual benefits of immigration when no means exists for undocumented persons who have lived, worked, and raised families here to become citizens. Without citizenship they earn lower wages, which means their tax burden is lower and they have less money to put back into the economy.

Not only would a restoration and regular updates of registry benefit the US economy, but the gradual naturalization of long-standing residents who lack legal status would offer relief from ever-expanding immigration enforcement budgets and a dangerous police state. The enforcement apparatus that mushroomed starting in 2003 has never served a purpose equal to its size or cost. A regularization of the undocumented population and a mechanism to ensure that long-term residents of the future do not live in legal limbo, as so many have since the 1980s, would force a reckoning with the outrageous size and cost of both ICE and CBP by permanently shrinking the number of undocumented persons in the country. These steps, especially in light of the dramatic post-2007 downturn in the size of the undocumented population and in unauthorized entries, would finally give the United States, after decades of deferring the problem, a sustainable way to deal with the reality of immigration. Less easily measured but of immense significance would be the moral credibility that comes with respecting immigrants' human rights.

A second important legislative element of any plan to rein in ICE and CBP requires Congress to reverse the disastrous laws passed in 1996: AEDPA and IIRIRA. DHS is a cabinet-level organization whose agencies are out of control in part because these two pieces of legislation demanded that immigration enforcement agencies treat immigrants who had not violated any laws as if they were hardened criminals. Repealing each law would remove a large part of the spurious justification for ICE's and CBP's massive growth and overreach.

The financial and human costs of AEDPA and IIRIRA have been astronomical. To reverse the criminalization of most undocumented immigrants, almost all of whom pose no threat to anyone, also requires reversing the Clinton-era changes that turned misdemeanors into deportable offenses. IIRIRA and AEDPA work together to criminalize immigrants who are not criminals. Doing so lines the pockets of private detention and electronic-surveillance companies and conveys to the public the false and pernicious impression that there is something illegal and dangerous about the idea of noncitizenship. ICE and CBP feed on this impression.

As long as aggravated felonies remain the basis for deportation orders, and as long as detention for many immigrants is mandatory, ICE and the private companies with which ICE contracts will keep writing themselves blank checks as they blow through already astronomical budgets and siphon money from other agencies. When the stakes are high for ICE, they are automatically high for CBP as well. Classifying aggravated felonies as deportable offenses and requiring mandatory detention for people whose only offenses, if they have committed any, are civil misdemeanors does nothing to enhance the safety and security of US citizens. These classifications have created a black hole into which taxpayer money has been poured for decades. They also embolden agencies in ways that have harmed both immigrants and citizens.

The first two steps I have identified—the revival of registry and the repeal of IIRIRA and AEDPA—both attack the over-reach of ICE and CBP by denying those agencies their targets and their mandate. These are measures to starve the beast. A final step to the process of regaining control of our immigration enforcement apparatus is to impose much stricter super-vision and penalties for lawless acts on these agencies, forcing them to focus their energies on the realities of immigration and immigrant incorporation. A nation claiming to respect the rule of law cannot tolerate a large, powerful paramilitary police force that answers to no court or disciplinary body. To begin the process of disciplining ICE and CBP, Congress should recombine ICE, CBP, and USCIS into one agency whose mandate is a well-functioning immigration system, not an incarceration-to-deportation pipeline.

What is a "well-functioning immigration system"? It is not a criminal justice system or a drug enforcement system. Those structures already exist. We do not need to duplicate either of them within the immigration system. A well-functioning immigration system respects US laws and people's rights. It focuses on keeping all people—immigrants and citizens—safe. A well-functioning immigration system has enough immigra-tion judges to thoroughly review in a timely fashion all the cases that need to be heard. At present, fewer than five hun-dred serve the entire country, even as ICE and CBP gain more staff, weapons, and detention facilities with each passing year. A well-functioning immigration system also puts resources into immigrant incorporation. Right now, of the billions DHS spends on everything from incarceration to military-grade weapons, only a few paltry million go toward helping eligible immigrants with the work of becoming citizens.[8]

Whereas updating registry and repealing IIRIRA and AEDPA will drastically reduce the population of people who are vulnerable to ICE's abuse and overreach, a thorough DHS-level reorganization would entirely reorient CBP, condensing and bringing into line this sprawling agency. At present and for the past few years, a large proportion of the people making their way to the southern border have been legally seeking asylum. We have every reason to believe this will be the case for the foreseeable future, even as we also know that this wave of arrivals will crest and recede, just as every wave prior has done. Short of closing borders, which would have devastating consequences for the US economy and nearly genocidal outcomes for people trying to flee violence and turmoil in Central America, asylum-seeking is a legal process that the United States must recognize.

But CBP has shown that it cannot be trusted with the consequential and delicate asylum process. Currently, CBP is supposed to refer asylum seekers to trained USCIS staff, who conduct interviews to determine if the seekers experience "credible fear" that would recommend against turning them away. This is only the first of the stages of vetting an asylum claim, but it is an important one. CBP has locked asylum seekers in "iceboxes," starved them, failed to inform them of their rights, neglected to refer them for an interview, and aggressively intimidated them.[9] If nothing else, immigration agencies and their agents should be required to respect the legal and fundamental human rights of immigrants. Resources could be allocated to relieving the bottlenecks in the process—providing enough trained staff to conduct responsible interviews and enough judges for immigration hearings.

Right now, the effects of the shortage of judges are exacerbated by the open campaign being waged by the Department of Justice to appoint immigrant-unfriendly judges. One preliminary analysis shows that more immigration judges come to the job from an immigration enforcement background than from any other profession, a fact that is correlated with lower rates of granting asylum claims.[10] Training for immigration judges is meager, and CBP has always focused on enforcement methods designed to exclude and deport, at the expense of due process. Dissolving CBP and replacing it with an organization that has adequate numbers of well-trained staff and a mandate to process asylum claims according to basic standards set by international human rights conventions would go a long way toward meeting the current needs of our southern border and attenuating the violent policing that occurs there.

Of the three proposals—updating registry, decriminalization, and agency reorganization—reorganization is in some ways the least politically ambitious. DHS is not an old, venerable institution. It was created, along with its subsidiary agencies, in a reactionary haste. The idea of a clean start resonates with many people who follow immigration policy and who believe that the severing of enforcement and removal work from more welcoming functions like naturalization and visa granting, all of which were performed by the INS before 2003, paved the way for enforcement to run amok. A subset of these experts also thinks that the authority structure of DHS failed to build in a means to properly oversee ICE and CBP, allowing unchecked bureaucracies to continually push for increases in their power and budgets in an effort to justify and secure their existence. Undoing the separation of USCIS and ICE/CBP would be cost-effective. More important, it would pave the way for the United States to once again treat immigrants as future citizens, as was our highly successful custom until recently, rather than as criminals.

I'VE TOLD THE story, in brief, of how our immigration regime burst out of the constraints that limit ordinary bureaucracies and became lawless. As it turns out, this is a story that affects not just immigrants but anyone in this country. Currently, our immigration agencies lock up and deport citizens, target journalists, spy on or track ordinary citizen protestors, and cooperate with violent, armed civilian militias. These institutions are not only out of control; they operate with impunity, ignoring even their own internal investigators. But they didn't become that way on their own. As was the case in the 1920s and 1930s, when Washington bureaucrats sent Border Patrol agents on invasive missions that borderland residents could see were pointless, and which frustrated them, the current politics of immigration enforcement are motivated by the objectives of people who reside far from the border and are willfully blind to the realities of contemporary immigration. White nationalists who stoke resentment of immigrants and stir up fear among ordinary Americans are enabled by politicians who fail to make sound policy. The minds of hardened nativists and racists probably cannot be changed. But we know from opinion polling that they do not represent most Americans. The rest of us can and should insist that Congress refuse to legislate based on white nationalist preferences.

Something that becomes clear when we talk about enforcement is that almost no one gets what they want when we pour substantial energy and resources into incarceration and deportation. At no point has enforcement been responsible for reducing the undocumented population in the United States or intimidating people who lack papers into staying away. Yet the costs to our rights and our budgets are high. Most worrisome is the degree to which our legal and constitutional rights are being compromised in the name of immigration enforcement.

As tempting as it is to think of citizens as immune to the atrocities being visited upon immigrants, in fact we should be very worried to see agents of our government empowered to break laws with impunity. If *some* laws can be disregarded, *all* laws can be, and what happens to immigrants can and will eventually happen to anyone, including citizens. If swift and dramatic policy action is not taken, the police state that ICE and CBP are building will only become further entrenched. Already we have seen the detention and deportation of US citizens, denationalizations, and significant costs to privacy. It is a shorter leap than one might imagine to a time when we're not just talking about sporadic raids or denaturalizing people who weren't born here, but about a state with the authority to revoke the citizenship of anyone, native born or otherwise. It is a shorter leap than you might think between taking away automatic citizenship for people born in the United States to noncitizen parents, and taking away the citizenship of people born in the country to convicted criminals, poor people, and others.

But until the fear and rage that have been stoked by nativists, white nationalist activists, and their rich, powerful benefactors are reined in by laws, policies, and institutions that prioritize rights over rage, we all remain vulnerable. The federal government should insist that our immigration bureaucracies focus their energies on ensuring that their agents respect the law instead of indiscriminately locking up and deporting as many immigrants as possible. The latter have proven too costly to everyone's rights. As long as ICE and CBP exist in their current form, our neighbors, coworkers, and family members, including those of us who are citizens, will need to wonder if and when we will hear an ominous knock at the door. Democracy isn't static. If a government can get away with objectionable actions against undocumented immigrants, what can stop it from attempting—and getting away with—repugnant actions against legal immigrants, then minority groups, then everyone?

Democracies don't just lose ground from the inside in obvious ways like electoral fraud; they erode at the edges, like a beach. Undocumented immigrants are on the shoreline of the land we all stand on. It may feel easy or even inevitable to accept that some—perhaps the most marginal, newly arrived, or vulnerable—wash away during turbulent times. But the forces that take them away will return, emboldened, and eventually will reach us all.

Acknowledgments

THE IDEA FOR A BRIEF, SERIOUS, YET ACCESSIBLE BOOK ABOUT immigration enforcement originated with Dan Gerstle, who came to me with the proposal via Corey Robin. I am indebted to them both for trusting me with this challenge. My agent, Susan Rabiner, helped craft the prospectus and advocated for the smartest possible version of the book. Lara Heimert at Basic Books took care to make sure the book has been supported, and Lisa Kaufman patiently edited my very rough drafts. Kelley Blewster copyedited with an extremely helpful eye for both form and substance, and Kaitlin Carruthers-Busser kept the production on track. Closer to home, Kelley Coleman and Sunju Raybeck provided invaluable support and good cheer.

This book (and I) have benefited immeasurably from the research and gentle incisive pushback of Nathan Yaffe, who assisted me while clerking on the Second Circuit and doing truly heroic volunteer immigrant advocacy. Abdulaziz Al-Sulaiti tracked down obscure sources, and Mary Grace Castle and Abby B. Raines provided invaluable technical help as I wrapped up. Carly Goodman has been incredibly generous about sharing her archival research on nativists and white nationalists. Cyril Ghosh has been my cherished friend and sounding board for almost twenty years now. He and I were finishing a different book when I started this one. He shouldered a fair bit of the endgame with that project, allowing me to start on this one.

My father, Ira J. Cohen, always wants the best for me and often reacts protectively when I float the idea of doing something surprising or risky. His cheerful support as I have plunged ahead with various endeavors he viewed with cautious skepticism means the world to me, as does he.

I wrote this book for Reggie Feiner Cohen, who is an immigrant, the very finest of citizens, and the most loving and loyal parent that I could imagine. I wrote it for her and because of her, for the world she has always worked for, and for the world she deserves to live in. People often talk about the arc of the moral universe bending toward justice, but the truth is that it does not bend on its own. It is bent by the morally courageous people who see injustice and cannot turn away. My mother is one of those rare people, bringing to every challenge a mind capable of observing crucial, innocuous-seeming details and discerning moral patterns that the rest of us overlook. Her warmth, intellect, and unwavering optimism transform everyone lucky enough to know her, most of all me. Our accomplishments are her accomplishments. This book is her book.

Notes

1. ENFORCEMENT GONE ROGUE

1. Jennifer Lynch, "From Finger Prints to DNA: Biometric Data Collection in U.S. Immigrant Communities and Beyond," American Immigration Council Special Report, May 2012, https://www.americanimmigration council.org/sites/default/files/research/lynch_-_biometrics_052112.pdf.

2. CBP San Diego (@CBPSanDiego), "Pedestrian crossings at the San Ysidro port of entry are also suspended at both the East and West facility," Twitter, November 25, 2018, 11:38 a.m., https://twitter.com/CBPSanDiego /status/1066778234501521408.

3. Ryan Devereaux, "Border Patrol Chief Carla Provost Was a Member of a Secret Facebook Group," The Intercept, July 12, 2019, https:// theintercept.com/2019/07/12/border-patrol-chief-carla-provost-was-a -member-of-secret-facebook-group/.

4. Avery Anapol, "Trump Told Border Official He'd Pardon Him if He Went to Jail over Immigration Moves: CNN," The Hill, April 12, 2019, https://thehill.com/latino/438683-trump-told-border-official-hed -pardon-him-if-he-went-to-jail-over-immigration-moves.

5. Jeffrey S. Passel and D'Vera Cohn, "Unauthorized Immigrant Population Stable for Half a Decade," Pew Research Center, September 21, 2016, https://www.pewresearch.org/fact-tank/2016/09/21/unauthorized-immigrant-population-stable-for-half-a-decade/.

6. Douglas Massey, "Today's US-Mexico 'Border Crisis' in 6 Charts," The Conversation, June 27, 2018, http://theconversation.com/todays-us-mexico-border-crisis-in-6-charts-98922.

7. 2030 is widely understood to be a tipping point, after which older people in the United States will outnumber younger people. The economic consequences of similar circumstances have been dramatic for countries like Italy and Japan.

8. Dave Mosher, "Mollie Tibbetts' Death Is Being Used to Push Debunked Ideas About Illegal Immigration and Violent Crime," Business Insider, August 22, 2018, https://www.businessinsider.com/undocumented-aliens-violent-crime-murder-statistics-data-2018-8.

9. Walter A. Ewing, Daniel E. Martinez, and Ruben G. Rumbaut, "The Criminalization of Immigration in the United States," American Immigration Council Special Report, July 2015, https://www.americanimmigrationcouncil.org/sites/default/files/research/the_criminalization_of_immigration_in_the_united_states.pdf.

10. TRAC Immigration, "Profiling Who ICE Detains: Few Committed Any Crime," TRAC Research Center Report, October 9, 2018, https://trac.syr.edu/immigration/reports/530/.

11. Daniel Denvir, "The Case Against 'Border Security,'" New York Times, February 11, 2019, https://www.nytimes.com/2019/02/11/opinion/democrats-border-security-wall.html. Denvir cites the following study: Leo Beletsky and Corey S. Davis, "Today's Fentanyl Crisis: Prohibition's Iron Law, Revisited," International Journal of Drug Policy 46 (August 2017): 156–159, doi:10.1016/j.drugpo.2017.05.050.

12. National Academics of Sciences, Engineering, and Medicine, "Immigration's Long-Term Impacts on Overall Wages and Employment of Native-Born U.S. Workers Very Small, Although Low-Skilled Workers May Be Affected, New Report Finds; Impacts on Economic Growth Positive, While Effects on Government Budgets Mixed," news release, September 21, 2016, http://www8.nationalacademies.org/onpinews/newsitem.aspx?RecordID=23550; Jordan Miriam, "8 Million People Are Working Illegally in the U.S. Here's Why That's Unlikely to Change," New York

Times, December 11, 2018, https://www.nytimes.com/2018/12/11/us /undocumented-immigrant-workers.html; "Kicking Out Immigrants Doesn't Raise Wages," *The Economist,* February 4, 2017, https://www .economist.com/united-states/2017/02/04/kicking-out-immigrants -doesnt-raise-wages?fsrc=scn/fb/te/bl/ed/kickingoutimmigrantsdoesnt raisewages.

13. American Association for the Advancement of Science, "Immigrants Use Little Health Care, Subsidize Care of Non-immigrants: Harvard/Tufts Study," news release, EurekAlert!, August 8, 2018, https:// www.eurekalert.org/pub_releases/2018-08/pfan-iul080718.php.

14. Michael Greenstone and Adam Looney, "Ten Economic Facts About Immigration," Hamilton Project Policy Memo, September 2010, https://www.brookings.edu/wp-content/uploads/2016/06/09_immigration.pdf.

15. A note on nomenclature: the term *white nationalist* is a contested one, as elucidated in Kathleen Belew's recent work on the subject. Belew sees the unifying theme of various hate and white nationalist groups as a commitment to white power. But she is talking about a larger set of ideologies and organizations than is directly relevant to the subject of this book. When I use the term *white nationalist* I generally do so with the belief in mind that the group or person to whom I refer seeks to make the United States a whiter nation. These individuals and organizations work with definitions of whiteness that change through the decades, but in all cases they view immigration through a hierarchical, racialized lens in which whiteness is prized. There are forms of nativism that are not white nationalist, although frequently the support for those forms of nativism is exploited by white nationalists. I therefore also refer to some groups and individuals as *nativist* when I believe it is possible to regard their anti-immigrant stance as one that is not primarily defined by a doctrine of white racial superiority.

16. Franklin Foer, "How Trump Radicalized ICE," *Atlantic,* September 2018, https://www.theatlantic.com/magazine/archive/2018/09/trump -ice/565772/.

17. Esha Bhandari and Hugh Handeyside, "The Government Is Detaining and Interrogating Journalists and Advocates at the US-Mexico Border," American Civil Liberties Union, March 7, 2019, https://www .aclu.org/blog/free-speech/freedom-press/government-detaining-and -interrogating-journalists-and-advocates-us.

18. Sam Levin, "University Charges Students for Protesting Against Border Patrol," *The Guardian,* April 3, 2019, https://www.theguardian.com /us-news/2019/apr/02/arizona-students-protest-border-patrol-charges.

19. Chris Rickerd, "Whistleblower Says CBP Has Culture of Impunity and Violence," American Civil Liberties Union, April 26, 2015, https:// www.aclu.org/blog/immigrants-rights/ice-and-border-patrol-abuses /whistleblower-says-cbp-has-culture-impunity-and?redirect=blog /whistleblower-says-cbp-has-culture-impunity-and-violence. Note that the surge in hiring in 2006–2009 led to some reforms, including the Anti–Border Corruption Act of 2010. Josiah Heyman, "Why Caution Is Needed Before Hiring Additional Border Patrol Agents and ICE Officers," American Immigration Council Special Report, April 2017, https://www.american immigrationcouncil.org/sites/default/files/research/why_caution_is _needed_before_hiring_additional_border_patrol_agents_and_ice_officers _final.pdf.

20. Justin Rohrlich and Zoë Schlanger, "Border Officers Are Arrested 5 Times More Often than Other US Law Enforcement," *Quartz,* July 16, 2019, https://qz.com/1664253/cbp-officers-arrested-5-times-as-often-as -other-law-enforcement/.

21. Gus Bova, "The Border Patrol Serial Killer Is Part of a Long, Troubled History," *Texas Observer,* September 19, 2018, https://www .texasobserver.org/the-border-patrol-serial-killer-is-part-of-a-long-troubled -history/.

22. Bova, "The Border Patrol Serial Killer Is Part of a Long, Troubled History."

23. Chris Rickerd, "Border Patrol Violence Must Stop," American Civil Liberties Union, June 5, 2015, https://www.aclu.org/blog/immigrants -rights/ice-and-border-patrol-abuses/border-patrol-violence-must-stop.

24. American Civil Liberties Union, "CBP Releases Deadly Force Report and Revised Use of Force Policies," news release, May 30, 2014, https://www.aclu.org/news/cbp-releases-deadly-force-report-and -revised-use-force-policies.

25. Note that the CBP maintains that it is appropriate to use lethal force when someone is throwing rocks. Bob Ortega and Rob O'Dell, "Deadly Border Agent Incidents Cloaked in Silence," *Azcentral,* March 28, 2014, https://www.azcentral.com/story/news/arizona/2014/03/28/arizona -border-force-deadly-incidents/7013023/.

26. Daniel Martinez, Guillermo Cantor, and Walter A. Ewing, "No Action Taken: Lack of CBP Accountability in Responding to Complaints of Abuse," American Immigration Council Special Report, July 18, 2015, https://ssrn.com/abstract=2633006.

27. Guillermo Cantor and Walter A. Ewing, "Still No Action Taken: Complaints Against Border Patrol Agents Continue to Go Unanswered," American Immigration Council Special Report, August 2017, https://www.americanimmigrationcouncil.org/sites/default/files/research/still_no_action_taken_complaints_against_border_patrol_agents_continue_to_go_unanswered.pdf.

28. Ortega and O'Dell, "Deadly Border Agent Incidents Cloaked in Silence."

29. American Civil Liberties Union, "Neglect and Abuse of Unaccompanied Immigrant Children by U.S. Customs and Border Protection," American Civil Liberties Union Report, May 2018, https://www.dropbox.com/s/lplnnufjbwci0xn/CBP%20Report%20ACLU_IHRC%205.23%20FINAL.pdf?dl=0.

30. Jonathan Blitzer, "The Border Patrol Was Primed for President Trump," *New Yorker,* February 17, 2017, https://www.newyorker.com/news/news-desk/the-border-patrol-was-primed-for-president-trump.

31. Jane Doe v. Various Defendants, United States District Court, W.D. Texas, El Paso Division (2013).

32. Alex Riggins, "CBP Officer Indicted on Charge of Strangling Traveler at San Ysidro Port of Entry," *San Diego Union-Tribune,* August 15, 2018, https://www.sandiegouniontribune.com/news/public-safety/sd-me-harvey-booker-indictment-20180815-story.html.

33. Aaron Rupar, "Migrant Girl Dies in Border Patrol's Custody," Vox, December 15, 2018, https://www.vox.com/policy-and-politics/2018/12/14/18140697/guatemalan-girl-dehydration-death-border-patrol-custody-dhs.

34. Hamed Aleaziz and Adolfo Flores, "A 16-Year-Old Unaccompanied Immigrant Boy Has Died in US Government Custody," BuzzFeed News, May 2, 2019, https://www.buzzfeednews.com/article/hamedaleaziz/unaccompanied-immigrant-boy-dies-us-custody.

35. Hannah Hafter et al., "Shakedown: How Deportation Robs Immigrants of Their Money and Belongings," No More Deaths's Property Recovery Assistance Project, December 2014, http://nomoredeaths.org/wp-content/uploads/2014/12/Shakedown-withcover.pdf.

36. Audrey McNamara, "FBI Arrests New Mexico Border Militia Leader Larry Mitchell Hopkins," *Daily Beast,* April 20, 2019, https://www.thedailybeast.com/fbi-arrests-larry-mitchell-hopkins-leader-of-united-constitutional-patriots-border-militia?via=twitter_page.

37. Ken Klippenstein, "'Put Them All in a Gas Chamber,' Said Border Militia Member: Report," TYT, May 6, 2019, https://tyt.com/stories/4vZLCHuQrYE4uKagy0oyMA/55ZimtgirWgUh9ZgMSPirI.

38. Kathleen Belew, *Bring the War Home: The White Power Movement and Paramilitary America* (Cambridge, MA: Harvard University Press, 2018), 43.

39. Belew, *Bring the War Home,* 106.

40. Belew, *Bring the War Home,* 78.

41. Eric Reidy, "Vigilantes Not Welcome: A Border Town Pushes Back on Anti-Immigrant Extremists," *Mother Jones,* May 2019, https://www.motherjones.com/politics/2019/04/immigrant-vigilantes-arizona-border-arivaca/.

42. Ryan Devereaux, "The Bloody History of Border Militias Runs Deep—and Law Enforcement Is Part of It," The Intercept, April 23, 2019, https://theintercept.com/2019/04/23/border-militia-migrants/.

43. Office for Civil Rights and Civil Liberties, "Quarterly Report to Congress, Third and Fourth Quarters, FY 2014," Department of Homeland Security, February 23, 2014, 4.

44. Alex Nowrasteh, "Border Patrol Termination Rates: Discipline and Performance Problems Signal Need for Reform," Policy Analysis No. 825, Cato Institute, November 2, 2017, https://object.cato.org/sites/cato.org/files/pubs/pdf/pa825.pdf.

45. Martin Garbus, "What I Saw at the Dilley, Texas, Immigrant Detention Center," *The Nation,* March 26, 2019, https://www.thenation.com/article/dilley-texas-immigration-detention/.

46. John V. Kelley, "Management Alert: DHS Needs to Address Dangerous Overcrowding Among Single Adults at El Paso Del Norte Processing Center," Memo, Office of the Inspector General to Kevin K. Aleenen, Acting Secretary, Department of Homeland Security, May 30, 2019, https://www.oig.dhs.gov/sites/default/files/assets/2019-05/OIG-19-46-May19.pdf.

47. Donald M. Kerwin and Serena Yi-Ying Lin, "Immigrant Detention: Can ICE Meet Its Legal Imperatives and Case Management Responsibilities?"

Migration Policy Institute, September 2009, p. 7, https://www.migrationpolicy
.org/research/immigrant-detention-can-ice-meet-its-legal-imperatives
-and-case-management-responsibilities.

48. J. Rachel Reyes, "Immigration Detention: Recent Trends and Scholarship," Center for Migration Studies, March 26, 2018, https://cmsny.org
/publications/virtualbrief-detention/.

49. Reyes, "Immigration Detention: Recent Trends and Scholarship."

50. Reyes, "Immigration Detention: Recent Trends and Scholarship."

51. Tal Kopan, "More than 14,000 Immigrant Children Are in U.S. Custody, An All-Time High," *San Francisco Chronicle,* November 16, 2018, https://www.sfchronicle.com/nation/article/More-than-14-000
-immigrant-children-are-in-U-S-13399510.php.

52. Dominique Mosbergen, "ICE Has Been Wrongly Detaining U.S. Citizens in Florida Jails, Says ACLU," Huffington Post, March 20, 2019, https://www.huffpost.com/entry/ice-detainers-miami-florida-aclu_n
_5c92c7c3e4b01b140d3536d9?ncid=engmodushpmg00000004.

53. David Bier, "U.S. Citizens Targeted by ICE: U.S. Citizens Targeted by Immigration and Customs Enforcement in Texas," Policy Brief No. 8, Cato Institute, August 29, 2018, https://www.cato.org/publications
/immigration-research-policy-brief/us-citizens-targeted-ice-us-citizens
-targeted.

54. ACLU Florida, "Citizens on Hold: A Look at ICE's Flawed Detainer System in Miami-Dade County," ACLU, March 20, 2019, https://
www.aclufl.org/en/publications/citizens-hold-look-ices-flawed-detainer
-system-miami-dade-county.

55. Hilary Hurd Anyaso, "Hundreds of U.S. Citizens Continue to Be Detained, New Immigration Data Shows," Analysis Report, Northwestern University's Deportation Research Clinic, August 10, 2017, https://news
.northwestern.edu/stories/2017/august/hundreds-of-u-s-citizens-continue
-to-be-detained-new-immigration-data-shows/.

56. Anyaso, "Hundreds of U.S. Citizens Continue to Be Detained, New Immigration Data Shows."

57. Alden Loury and Maria Ines Zamudio, "O'Hare Standoff Over: Federal Officials Release Three Children to Undocumented Mother," WBEZ News, July 18, 2019, https://www.wbez.org/shows/wbez-news
/ohare-standoff-border-patrol-detaining-three-children-of-undocumented
-parents/285e32de-2516-4be2-b660-fd7b0419e913.

58. United States Government Database, Executive Office for Immigration Review, Office of Planning, Analysis, and Statistics, "Certain Criminal Charge Completion Statistics," August 2016, https://www.justice.gov/sites/default/files/pages/attachments/2016/08/25/criminal-charge-completion-statistics-201608.pdf.

59. Kari Paul, "Advocates Say the Fastest Way to Help Immigrants Separated from Their Children: Post Their Bail," Market Watch, August 16, 2018, https://www.marketwatch.com/story/this-is-what-it-costs-to-free-one-immigrant-from-detention-2018-06-20.

60. Ingrid Eagly, Steven Shafer, and Jana Whalley, "Detaining Families: A Study of Asylum Adjudication in Family Detention," American Immigration Council Special Report, August 16, 2018, https://www.americanimmigrationcouncil.org/research/detaining-families-a-study-of-asylum-adjudication-in-family-detention.

61. Matthew La Corte, "Restore the Family Case Management Program for Asylum Seekers," Niskanen Center, April 17, 2019, https://niskanencenter.org/blog/restore-the-family-case-management-program-for-asylum-seekers/.

62. New York Civil Liberties Union, "Lawsuit Challenges Unlawful Detention of Asylum-Seekers at Buffalo Immigration Jail," press release, September 26, 2017, https://www.nyclu.org/en/press-releases/lawsuit-challenges-unlawful-detention-asylum-seekers-buffalo-immigration-jail (noting that after President Trump's inauguration, parole rates at the facility fell from about 50 percent to about 10 percent). See also Abdi v. Duke, 280 F. Supp. 3d 373 (W.D.N.Y. 2017) (finding that the government violated parole eligibility rules, ordering the government to comply with the parole directive, and ordering individualized bond hearings for arriving asylum seekers after six months in detention).

63. David Jennings v. Alejandro Rodriguez, 583 U.S. 5 (2018), https://www.scotusblog.com/wp-content/uploads/2016/10/15-1204_amicus_resp_american_immigration_council_et_al.pdf.

64. Ingrid Eagly and Steven Shafer, "A National Study of Access to Counsel in Immigration Court," *University of Pennsylvania Law Review* 164, no. 1 (December 2015), Table 6, https://scholarship.law.upenn.edu/cgi/viewcontent.cgi?article=9502&context=penn_law_review.

65. Alice Speri, "Detained, Then Violated," The Intercept, April 11, 2018, https://theintercept.com/2018/04/11/immigration-detention-sexual-abuse-ice-dhs/.

66. Speri, "Detained, Then Violated."

67. Speri, "Detained, Then Violated."

68. Alice Speri, "At Largest ICE Detention Center in the Country, Guards Called Attempted Suicides 'Failures,'" The Intercept, October 11, 2018, https://theintercept.com/2018/10/11/adelanto-ice-detention-center-abuse/.

69. Lisa Riordan Seville, Hannah Rappleye, and Andrew W. Lehren, "22 Immigrants Died in ICE Detention Centers During the Past 2 Years," NBC News, January 6, 2019, https://www.nbcnews.com/politics/immigration/22-immigrants-died-ice-detention-centers-during-past-2-years-n954781.

70. Ken Klippenstein, "ICE Stopped Updating Its List of 'Deaths in ICE Custody,'" TYT, June 17, 2019, https://tyt.com/stories/4vZLCHuQrYE4uKagy0oyMA/2rdpMiN8dW4CwMxQisARTm.

71. Department of Homeland Security Office of Inspector General, "ICE Does Not Fully Use Contracting Tools to Hold Detention Facility Contractors Accountable for Failing to Meet Performance Standards," January 29, 2019, https://www.oig.dhs.gov/sites/default/files/assets/2019-02/OIG-19-18-Jan19.pdf.

72. Noah Lanard, "ICE Just Quietly Opened Three New Detention Centers, Flouting Congress' Limits," Mother Jones, July 9, 2019, https://www.motherjones.com/politics/2019/07/ice-just-quietly-opened-three-new-detention-centers-flouting-congress-limits/.

73. Unaccompanied minors, including those who are forcibly separated from parents by ICE and CBP, are referred to the Office of Refugee Resettlement, which either incarcerates them or places them in the care of sponsors.

74. Matthew Haag, "Thousands of Immigrant Children Said They Were Sexually Abused in U.S. Detention Centers, Report Says," New York Times, February 27, 2019, https://www.nytimes.com/2019/02/27/us/immigrant-children-sexual-abuse.html?smid=nytcore-ios-share.

75. Jess Bidgood, Manny Fernandez, and Richard Fausset, "Restraint Chairs and Spit Masks: Migrant Detainees Claim Abuse at Detention

Centers," *New York Times,* August 4, 2018, https://www.nytimes.com /2018/08/04/us/migrant-children-detention-centers.html.

76. Doe 4 v. Shenandoah Valley Juvenile Center Commission, 171 W.D. Va. (2018).

77. "U.S. Centers Force Migrant Children to Take Drugs: Lawsuit," Reuters, June 20, 2018, https://www.reuters.com/article/us-usa-immigration -medication/u-s-centers-force-migrant-children-to-take-drugs-lawsuit -idUSKBN1JH076.

78. Catherine E. Shoichet and Edith Bracho-Sanchez, "These Doctors Risked Their Careers to Expose the Dangers Children Face in Immigrant Family Detention," CNN, May 23, 2019, https://www.cnn.com/2019/05/23 /health/ice-family-detention-whistleblowers-doctors/index.html.

79. Ema O'Connor and Nidhi Prakash, "Pregnant Women Say They Miscarried in Immigration Detention and Didn't Get the Care They Needed," BuzzFeed News, July 9, 2018, https://www.buzzfeednews.com /article/emaoconnor/pregnant-migrant-women-miscarriage-cpb-ice -detention-trump.

80. Opheli Garcia Lawler, "Nearly 30 Women Have Miscarried While Detained by ICE Since 2017," The Cut, March 4, 2019, https://www.thecut .com/2019/03/nearly-30-women-miscarried-while-detained-by-ice-since -2017.html.

81. Casey Delehanty, Jack Mewhirter, Ryan Welch, and Jason Wilks, "Militarization and Police Violence: The Case of the 1033 Program," *Research and Politics* 4, no. 2 (June 14, 2017): 1–7, doi:10.1177/2053168017712885.

82. Alex S. Vitale, "How to End Militarized Policing," *The Nation,* August 18, 2014, https://www.thenation.com/article/how-end-militarized-policing/.

83. Josiah Heyman, "Why Caution Is Needed Before Hiring Additional Border Patrol Agents and ICE Officers," American Immigration Council Special Report, April 2017, https://www.americanimmigrationcouncil .org/sites/default/files/research/why_caution_is_needed_before_hiring _additional_border_patrol_agents_and_ice_officers_final.pdf.

84. Department of Homeland Security Office of Inspector General, "Assaults on CBP and ICE Law Enforcement Officers," September 4, 2018, https://www.oig.dhs.gov/sites/default/files/assets/2018-09/OIG-18-76 -Sep18.pdf.

85. Debbie Nathan, "How the Border Patrol Faked Statistics Showing a 73 Percent Rise in Assaults Against Agents," The Intercept, April 23, 2018, https://theintercept.com/2018/04/23/border-patrol-agents-assaulted-cbp-fbi/. See also Debbie Nathan, "Border Patrol Continues to Exaggerate Danger to Agents to Justify Violence Against Immigrants," The Intercept, June 1, 2018, https://theintercept.com/2018/06/01/border-patrol-agent-assault-statistics-fbi/.

86. Department of Homeland Security Office of Inspector General, "Assaults on CBP and ICE Law Enforcement Officers."

87. Department of Homeland Security Office of Inspector General, "Assaults on CBP and ICE Law Enforcement Officers."

88. Alex Nowrasteh, "Border Patrol Agent Deaths in the Line of Duty," Cato Institute, November 27, 2017, https://www.cato.org/blog/border-patrol-agent-deaths-line-duty.

89. Miami Herald Editorial Board, "Trump's Tragedy at the Border Just Won't End—By Design," *Miami Herald*, February 9, 2019, https://www.miamiherald.com/opinion/editorials/article226019160.html.

90. Sarah McCammon and Teri Schultz, "News Brief: Trump and EU Ease Trade Tensions, Family Separation Update," Morning Edition, National Public Radio, July 26, 2018.

91. Miriam Jordan, "Family Separation May Have Hit Thousands More Migrant Children than Reported," *New York Times*, January 17, 2019, https://www.nytimes.com/2019/01/17/us/family-separation-trump-administration-migrants.html.

92. EJ Montini, "The Feds Lost—Yes, Lost—1,475 Migrant Children," *USA Today*, May 25, 2018, https://www.usatoday.com/story/opinion/nation-now/2018/05/25/immigration-children-separated-families-lost-column/643793002/?fbclid=IwAR058ooVrCGUFL80i8SLbVYIQq0sMEQbjL9p5i6kUZ_XfkC_i-lKBMVFbZ8.

93. United States Government Accountability Office, "Components Could Improve Monitoring of the Employee Misconduct Process," Report to Congressional Requesters, July 2018, https://www.hsdl.org/?view&did=814952. For the last three years for which records are available, CBP reports total use-of-force incidents as follows—FY2015: 752 incidents; FY2016: 973 incidents; FY2017: 996 incidents.

94. Police Executive Research Forum, "U.S. Customs and Border Protection—Use of Force Review," February 2013, https://www.cbp.gov/sites/default/files/documents/PERFReport.pdf.

95. Frank Newport and Riley Brands, "Gallup Review: Americans, Immigration and the Election," Gallup News, October 27, 2016, https://news.gallup.com/opinion/polling-matters/196733/gallup-review-americans-immigration-election.aspx.

96. Alfredo Corchado, "Immigration Reform Is Rooted in Texas Views, Pollsters Conclude," *Dallas News,* September 11, 2018, https://www.dallasnews.com/news/immigration/2018/09/11/immigration-reform-rooted-texas-views-pollsters-conclude.

97. Julia Toepfer and Tara Tidwell Cullen, "ICE Lies, Manipulates, and Takes Money from Other Agencies to Lock Up and Deport More Immigrants," National Migrant Justice Center Report, September 2018, https://immigrantjustice.org/staff/blog/ice-lies-manipulates-and-takes-money-other-agencies-lock-and-deport-more-immigrants.

98. Hamed Aleaziz, "Civil Servants Who Process Immigration Applications Are Being Asked to Help ICE Instead," BuzzFeed News, July 17, 2019, https://www.buzzfeednews.com/article/hamedaleaziz/uscis-immigration-applications-backlog-ice.

99. Arthur Villasanta, "Pentagon to Transfer $1B to Fund Trump's Border Wall Despite Congress' Outrage," *International Business Times,* March 27, 2019, https://www.ibtimes.com/pentagon-transfer-1b-fund-trumps-border-wall-despite-congress-outrage-2780480.

100. Molly O'Toole (@mollymotoole), "ICE ~50k detention pop costs roughly $5m/day," Twitter, March 14, 2019, 2:25 p.m., https://twitter.com/mollymotoole/status/1106305279862411270?s=20.

101. Aaron Reichlin-Melnick (@ReichlinMelnick), "The $5 million a day estimate here for ICE detention is actually low. Last year ICE said a detention bed cost $123.86/day. So at 50k current average daily population, ICE is paying $6.2 million/day. When you account for around ~2500 family detention beds it's $6.7 million/day," Twitter, March 14, 2019, 3:21 p.m., https://twitter.com/ReichlinMelnick/status/1106319440424198144?s=20.

102. CBS, "The Billion-Dollar Industry of Detaining Immigrant Children," CBS News, July 13, 2018, https://www.cbsnews.com/news/the-billion-dollar-industry-of-detaining-immigrant-kids/.

103. Caitlin Dickerson, "Detention of Migrant Children Has Sky-rocketed to Highest Levels Ever," *New York Times*, September 12, 2018, https://www.nytimes.com/2018/09/12/us/migrant-children-detention .html?smtyp=cur&smid=tw-nytimes.

104. Kim Barker, Nicholas Kulish, and Rebecca R. Ruiz, "He's Built an Empire, with Detained Migrant Children as the Bricks," *New York Times*, December 2, 2018, https://www.nytimes.com/2018/12/02/us/southwest -key-migrant-children.html.

105. Maria Sacchetti, "Former Southwest Key Leader Who Ran Migrant Child Shelters for U.S. Government Earned $3.6 Million in 2017," *Washington Post*, July 13, 2019, https://www.washingtonpost .com/immigration/former-southwest-key-leader-who-ran-migrant-child-shelters-for-us-government-earned-36-million-in-2017/2019/07/13 /932d3738-a4a9-11e9-b732-41a79c2551bf_story.html?noredirect=on&utm _term=.5e538132dbd9.

106. Michael D. Shear and Emmarie Huetteman, "Trump Insists Mexico Will Pay for Wall After U.S. Begins the Work," *New York Times*, January 6, 2017, https://www.nytimes.com/2017/01/06/us/politics/trump -wall-mexico.html.

107. DHS gave an estimate of $21 billion. Vanda Felbab-Brown, "The Wall: The Real Cost of the Barrier Between the United States and Mexico," Brookings Report, August, 2017, https://www.brookings.edu/essay/the -wall-the-real-costs-of-a-barrier-between-the-united-states-and-mexico/.

108. David Willman, "Times Investigation: Trump Administration Has Gutted Programs Aimed at Detecting Weapons of Mass Destruction," *Los Angeles Times*, July 18, 2019, https://www.latimes.com/politics /story/2019-07-17/times-investigation-homeland-security-gutted-programs -aimed-at-stopping-wmd-terrorism.

109. Washington Post Editorial Board, "Immigrants Aren't Terrorists, No Matter What the Administration Says," *Washington Post*, January 4, 2019, https://www.washingtonpost.com/opinions/immigrants-arent -terrorists-no-matter-what-the-administration-says/2019/01/04/1ce64cfa -105b-11e9-8938-5898adc28fa2_story.html?utm_term=.a487b4745512.

110. Alex Nowrasteh, "Center for Immigration Studies Shows a Very Small Threat from Terrorists Crossing the Mexican Border," Cato Institute, November 28, 2018, https://www.cato.org/blog/center-immigration -studies-shows-very-small-threat-terrorists-crossing-mexican-border.

111. Department of Homeland Security, "Homeland Security Investigations for the Honorable Secretary Kirstjen Nielsen," US Immigration and Customs Enforcement, June 2018.

2. CONSTITUTIONALLY UNSHACKLED

1. "An Act to amend the law relating to the authority of certain employees of the Immigration and Naturalization Service . . . ," 79th Cong., 2nd Sess., Chapter 768 (1946), https://www.loc.gov/law/help/statutes-at -large/79th-congress/session-2/c79s2ch769.pdf.

2. 8 C.F.R. §287.1 (a)(2).

3. Brendlin v. California, 551 U.S. 249, 251 (2007).

4. 8 C.F.R. §287.1 (a)(2).

5. Any vehicle stop constitutes a "seizure" for Fourth Amendment purposes. Brendlin v. California.

6. United States v. Montoya de Hernandez, 473 U.S. 531, 538 (1985) ("Routine searches of the persons and effects of entrants are not subject to any requirement of reasonable suspicion, probable cause, or warrant"). To go beyond a "routine" search, the court requires "reasonable suspicion." United States v. Montoya de Hernandez, 541 ("We hold that the detention of a traveler at the border, beyond the scope of a routine customs search and inspection, is justified at its inception if customs agents, considering all the facts surrounding the traveler and her trip, reasonably suspect that the traveler is smuggling contraband in her alimentary canal").

7. United States v. Brignoni-Ponce, 422 U.S. 873, 884, 95 S. Ct. 2574, 2582, 45 L. Ed. 2d 607 (1975).

8. United States v. Brignoni-Ponce, 886. Note, however, that in United States v. Montero-Camargo, 208 F.3d 1122, 1132 (9th Cir. 2000), the Ninth Circuit held that "Hispanic appearance" is not an "appropriate factor." United States v. Montero-Camargo, 208 F.3d 1122, 1132 (9th Cir. 2000).

9. Amy B. Wang, "Two Americans Were Detained by a Border Patrol Agent After He Heard Them Speaking Spanish," *Washington Post*, May 21, 2018, https://www.washingtonpost.com/news/post-nation/wp/2018/05 /20/a-border-patrol-agent-detained-two-u-s-citizens-at-a-gas-station -after-hearing-them-speak-spanish/?utm_term=.fb5e1959066d.

10. New York Civil Liberties Union, "Justice Derailed: What Raids on New York's Trains and Buses Reveal About Border Patrol's Interior En-

forcement Practices," New York Civil Liberties Union, NYU School of Law Immigration Rights Clinic, FFF, November 2011, https://www.law.nyu .edu/sites/default/files/upload_documents/Justice%20Derailed.pdf.

11. James Lyall, staff attorney, ACLU of Arizona, letter to Tamara Kessler and Charles K. Edwards, Department of Homeland Security, "Complaint and Request for Investigation of Abuses at U.S. Border Patrol Interior Checkpoints in Southern Arizona, Including Unlawful Search and Seizure, Excessive Force, and Racial Profiling," January 15, 2014, https://www.aclusandiego.org/wp-content/uploads/2014/11/ACLU-AZ -Complaint-re-CBP-Checkpoints-2014-01-15.pdf.

12. Quoted in Tanvi Misra, "Inside the Massive U.S. 'Border Zone,'" City Lab, May 14, 2018, https://www.citylab.com/equity/2018/05/who -lives-in-border-patrols-100-mile-zone-probably-you-mapped/558275/.

13. Todd Miller, "War on the Border," *New York Times,* August 17, 2013, https://www.nytimes.com/2013/08/18/opinion/sunday/war-on-the -border.html?pagewanted=all&_r=0.

14. Christian Britschgi, "Border Control Installs Camera on Man's Property Without Asking. When He Takes It Down, They Demand It Back. Now He's Suing," *Hit and Run Blog,* February 27, 2018, https://reason.com /blog/2018/02/27/man-snatches-border-patrols-camera-left.

15. See IIRIRA §102(c)(1), as amended.

16. United States Government Accountability Office, "Secure Border Initiative: Observations on the Importance of Applying Lessons Learned to Future Projects," statement of Richard M. Stana, Director, Homeland Security and Justice Issues, February 2008, https://www.gao.gov/assets /120/119064.pdf.

17. T. Christian Miller, Kiah Collier, and Julián Aguilar, "The Taking," ProPublica, December 14, 2017, https://features.propublica.org /eminent-domain-and-the-wall/the-taking-texas-government-property -seizure/.

18. Note that the Senate Homeland Security and Governmental Affairs Committee Minority Report puts the number of lawsuits over condemnation actions at 330. Miller, Collier, and Aguilar, "The Taking."

19. Nomaan Merchant, "As Wall Looms, US Moves to Settle Border Fence Land Cases," NBC Chicago, June 16, 2017, https://www.nbcchicago .com/news/national-international/Wall-Looms-US-Moves-Settle-Border -Fence-Land-Cases-428921963.html. See also Vanda Felbab-Brown, "The

Wall: The Real Costs of a Barrier Between the United States and Mexico," Brookings Report, August 2017, https://www.brookings.edu/essay/the-wall-the-real-costs-of-a-barrier-between-the-united-states-and-mexico/.

20. "Trump Border Wall: Texans Receiving Letters About Their Land," CBS News, March 15, 2017, https://www.cbsnews.com/news/trump-border-wall-texans-receiving-letters-about-their-land/.

21. "Texans Get First Land Notices for Trump's Border Wall," Daily Beast, updated April 11, 2017, https://www.thedailybeast.com/texans-get-first-land-notices-for-trumps-border-wall.

22. *Building America's Trust Through Border Security: Progress on the Southern Border, Before the Committee of the Judiciary,* 115th Congress (2017) (statement of Mazie Hirono, Senator of the United States).

23. Lauren Carasik, "The Government Is Targeting Immigration Lawyers, Activists, and Reporters," *Boston Review,* April 24, 2019, http://bostonreview.net/global-justice/lauren-carasik-government-targeting-immigration-lawyers-activists-journalists.

24. Rekha Sharma-Crawford and Genevra Alberti, "Practice Advisory: Challenging the Constitutionality (or Legality) of Stipulated Removal Orders Issued Between 1997 and 2012 in Reinstatement and 8 U.S.C. §1326 Cases," Sharma-Crawford, Attorneys at Law, accessed July 22, 2019, https://sharma-crawford.com/wp-content/uploads/2018/10/Practice-Advisory-FINAL-10-03-2018.pdf.

25. Jennifer Lee Koh, "When Shadow Removals Collide: Searching for Solutions to the Legal Black Holes Created by Expedited Removal and Reinstatement," *Washington University Law Review* 96, no. 2 (2018): 341, https://wustllawreview.org/wp-content/uploads/12.-Koh-Final.pdf.

26. Cynthia Mehta and Lin Walker, "Reinstatement of Removal," Immigration Daily, 2005, https://www.ilw.com/articles/2005,0526-mehta.shtm.

27. Ingrid Eagly and Steven Shafer, "Access to Counsel in Immigration Court," American Immigration Council Special Report, September 2016, https://www.americanimmigrationcouncil.org/research/access-counsel-immigration-court.

28. Arelis R. Hernandez, "Judge Halts Mother-Daughter Deportation, Threatens to Hold Sessions in Contempt," *Washington Post,* August 9, 2018, https://www.washingtonpost.com/local/immigration/judge-halts-mother-daughter-deportation-threatens-to-hold-sessions-in-contempt/2018

/08/09/a23a0580-9bd6-11e8-8d5e-c6c594024954_story.html?utm_term= .defc1b669931.

29. Innovation Law Lab v. Nielsen, Case No. 3:18-cv-01098-SI (D. Or. June 25, 2018).

30. Dan Canon, "A System Designed to Make People Disappear," Slate, April 2, 2017, http://www.slate.com/articles/news_and_politics/cover _story/2017/04/ice_detainees_enter_an_unbelievably_cruel_system _designed_to_make_them_disappear.html?via=gdpr-consent.

31. Daniel Denvir, "The Roots of Trump's Immigration Barbarity," *Jacobin Magazine*, June 20, 2018, https://www.jacobinmag.com/2018/06 /trump-immigration-child-family-separation-policy.

32. Jeffrey S. Chase, "Attorneys and Credible Fear Review," *Jeffrey S. Chase Opinions/Analysis on Immigration Law* (blog), July 22, 2018, https:// www.jeffreyschase.com/blog/2018/7/22/attorneys-and-credible-fear-review.

33. Jennifer Lee Koh, Jayashri Srikantiah, and Karen C. Tumlin, "Deportation Without Due Process," National Immigration Law Center, September 2011, https://www.nilc.org/wp-content/uploads/2016/02 /Deportation-Without-Due-Process-2011-09.pdf.

34. Jeffrey S. Chase, "Matter of J-C-H-F-: An Interesting Omission," *Jeffrey S. Chase Opinions/Analysis on Immigration Law* (blog), March 2, 2018, https://www.jeffreyschase.com/blog/2018/3/2/matter-of-j-c-h-f-an -interesting-omission.

35. TRAC Immigration, "Newly Arriving Families Not Main Reason for Immigration Court's Growing Backlog," TRAC Research Center Report, March 18, 2019, https://trac.syr.edu/immigration/reports/551/; Daniel M. Kowalski, "Immigration Court Backlog Surpasses One Million Cases—TRAC Report," LexisNexis, November 6, 2018, https:// www.lexisnexis.com/legalnewsroom/immigration/b/outsidenews/posts /immigration-court-backlog-surpasses-one-million-cases—trac-report; Cristobal Ramon and Tim O'Shea, "Why Hiring More Judges Would Reduce Immigration Court Backlogs," Bipartisan Policy Center, July 25, 2018, https://bipartisanpolicy.org/blog/why-hiring-more-judges-would -reduce-immigration-court-backlogs/.

36. TRAC Immigration, "Burgeoning Immigration Judge Workloads," May 23, 2019, https://trac.syr.edu/immigration/reports/558/.

37. Hamed Aleaziz, "Immigration Judges Have Been Told to Hold More Hearings," BuzzFeed News, August 23, 2018, https://

www.buzzfeednews.com/article/hamedaleaziz/immigration-judges
-have-been-told-to-hold-more-hearings.

38. TRAC Immigration, "Findings of Credible Fear Plummet amid Widely Disparate Outcomes by Location and Judge," July 30, 2018, https://trac.syr.edu/immigration/reports/523/.

39. Dara Lind (@DLind), "January saw the imposition of this standard," Twitter, July 30, 2018, 12:16 p.m., https://twitter.com/DLind/status /1024010909730201601.

40. Greg Jaffe, Missy Ryan, and Nick Miroff, "Pentagon Set to Expand Military Role Along Southern Border," *Washington Post,* April 26, 2018, https://www.washingtonpost.com/world/national-security/pentagon-set -to-expand-military-role-along-southern-border/2019/04/26/f2b04666 -682a-11e9-82ba-fcfeff232e8f_story.html?utm_term=.ecade275b997.

41. Tal Kopan, "Trump's New Attorney General Launches Fresh Changes to Immigration Courts," *San Francisco Chronicle,* April 12, 2019, https://www.sfchronicle.com/politics/article/Trump-s-new-attorney -general-launches-fresh-13761430.php.

42. Kopan, "Trump's New Attorney General Launches Fresh Changes to Immigration Courts."

43. Mark A. Drummond, "'Death Penalty Cases in a Traffic Court Setting': Lessons from the Front Lines of Today's Immigration Courts," American Bar Association, January 15, 2019, https://www.americanbar.org /groups/litigation/publications/litigation-news/practice-points/death -penalty-cases-traffic-court-setting-lessons-front-lines-immigration-courts/.

44. Rachel McGonagill (@rachelmcgonagi1), "There's nowhere else in our system," Twitter, April 19, 2019, 7:47 a.m., https://twitter.com /RachelMcGonagi1/status/1119251120264630272/photo/1.

45. Tom Hals, "Groups Sue U.S. to Stop Deportation Hearings by Video-conference in New York," Reuters, February 13, 2019, https://www.reuters .com/article/us-usa-immigration-lawsuit/groups-sue-u-s-to-stop -deportation-hearings-by-videoconference-in-new-york-idUSKCN1Q22FJ ?feedType=RSS&feedName=domesticNews.

46. Tal Kopan, "Videos Start Replacing Interpreters at Immigration Court Hearings," *San Francisco Chronicle,* July 17, 2019, https://www.sfchronicle.com/news/article/Videos-start-replacing-interpreters -at-14103649.php?psid=dbHfi.

47. Matter of Castro-Tum, 27 I&N Dec. 271 (A.G. 2018).

48. "ICE Criminal Offense Levels Business Rules," table, TRAC Immigration Reports, April 24, 2013, https://trac.syr.edu/immigration/reports/330/include/DocumentReleased_13-15734_Criminal_Offense_Level_Business_Rules.pdf.

49. Ashleigh Atwell, "Philadelphia Native Sues ICE After They Tried Deporting Him to Jamaica," Blavity, December 2018, https://blavity.com/philadelphia-native-sues-ice-after-they-tried-deporting-him-to-jamaica?fbclid=IwAR0f96D5o1jlwbN0_SFj5jOnPIhK_XQ_eCDiR866x47IbwMqLPxVcBzqUts.

50. Niraj Warikoo, "Marine's Mom: My Son Is a U.S. Citizen, Why Was He Detained by ICE?" *Detroit Free Press,* January 17, 2019, https://www.freep.com/story/news/2019/01/17/ice-marines-veteran-jilmar-ramos-gomez-michigan/2595955002/.

51. Darlena Cunha, "ICE Is Dangerously Inaccurate," *New York Times,* July 12, 2019, https://www.nytimes.com/2019/07/12/opinion/ice-raids.html.

52. Darlena Cunha, "ICE Is Dangerously Inaccurate."

53. Bianca Bruno, "Ninth Circuit Says Government Must Bear the Burden of Determining Citizenship," Courthouse News Service, November 30, 2018, https://www.courthousenews.com/ninth-circuit-says-government-must-bear-the-burden-of-determining-citizenship/?fbclid=IwAR0Yro0iZYteizzB__e01BAFzsJrJiUQi2WTd3tT0k4iwuTSD_PGZjCVK3Y.

54. Ignacio Lanuza v. Johnathan M. Love, United States Court of Appeals for the Ninth Circuit, Seattle, Washington (2018).

55. Scott Bixby, "Deported to the Wrong Country—For a Crime He May Not Have Committed," Daily Beast, April 25, 2019, https://www.thedailybeast.com/deported-for-a-crime-he-didnt-committo-the-wrong-country.

56. Jeff Gammage, "Adopted Years Ago, Thousands Learn They Are Not U.S. Citizens," *Philadelphia Inquirer,* April 4, 2017, https://www.inquirer.com/philly/news/Adopted-from-Vietnam-as-a-baby—but-told-shes-not-an-American-citizen.html.

57. Tara Copp, "Adopted Daughter of Military Family Will Have to Leave the Country, Court Rules," *Military Times,* October 1, 2018, https://www.militarytimes.com/news/your-military/2018/10/01/adopted-daughter-of-military-family-will-have-to-leave-the-country-court-rules/?fbclid=IwAR1Okeq1cuODaRbwkAuzH1FCcVPG3_IorgsEKPvPUBgRRQzkJCLfPyr8eeU#.XLeC8NiF_bi.facebook.

58. Brennan Center for Justice, "Citizens Without Proof: A Survey of Americans' Possession of Documentary Proof of Citizenship and Photo Identification," Voting Rights and Elections Series at NYU School of Law, November 28, 2006, https://www.brennancenter.org/analysis/citizens -without-proof.

59. Patrick Weil, *The Sovereign Citizen Denaturalization and the Origins of the American Republic* (Philadelphia: University of Pennsylvania Press, 2012).

60. Jie Zong, Jeanne Batalova, and Micayla Burrows, "Frequently Requested Statistics on Immigrants and Immigration in the United States," Migration Policy Institute, March 14, 2019, https://www.migrationpolicy .org/article/frequently-requested-statistics-immigrants-and-immigration -united-states#Naturalization. Only those with dual citizenship can be denaturalized. It is very difficult to estimate the percentage of the naturalized population that has dual citizenship, but retaining one's original citizenship after naturalizing in the United States has become common since it was made legal in 1967.

61. Eric Schmitt, "U.S. Is Seeking to Strip 5,000 of Citizenship," *New York Times,* May 24, 1997, https://www.nytimes.com/1997/05/24/us/us-is -seeking-to-strip-5000-of-citizenship.html?mtrref=undefined&gwh=2502 EE235D46D10B19663CEC53E56BF9&gwt=pay.

62. Jon B. Hultman, "Administrative Denaturalization: Is There Nothing You Can Do That Can't Be [Un]Done," *Loyola of Los Angeles Law Review* 34 (2001): 895.

63. Revocation of naturalization, 8 U.S.C. § 1451 (2011).

64. The body responsible for implementing Operation Second Look is United States Citizenship and Immigration Services (USCIS), a DHS agency.

65. Seth Freed Wessler, "Is Denaturalization the Next Front in the Trump Administration's War on Immigration?" *New York Times,* December 19, 2018, https://www.nytimes.com/2018/12/19/magazine/naturalized -citizenship-immigration-trump.html.

66. Wessler, "Is Denaturalization the Next Front in the Trump Administration's War on Immigration?"

67. Nick Miroff, "Scanning Immigrants' Old Fingerprints, U.S. Threatens to Strip Thousands of Citizenship," *Chicago Tribune,* June 13, 2018,

https://www.chicagotribune.com/news/nationworld/ct-trump-immigration-strip-citizenship-20180613-story.html.

68. Department of Homeland Security, "Privacy Impact Assessment for the Automated Biometric Identification System," Automated Biometric Identification System (IDENT), December 7, 2012, https://www.dhs.gov/sites/default/files/publications/privacy-pia-nppd-ident-06252013.pdf.

69. https://www.dhs.gov/sites/default/files/publications/U.S.%20Immigration%20and%20Customs%20Enforcement.pdf.

70. Department of Homeland Security, "FY 2019 Budget in Brief."

71. Masha Gessen, "In America, Naturalized Citizens No Longer Have an Assumption of Permanence," *New Yorker*, June 18, 2018, https://www.newyorker.com/news/our-columnists/in-america-naturalized-citizens-no-longer-have-an-assumption-of-permanence.

72. Adiel Kaplan, "Miami Grandma Targeted as U.S. Takes Aim at Naturalized Immigrants with Prior Offenses," *Miami Herald*, July 9, 2018, https://www.miamiherald.com/news/local/immigration/article214173489.html.

73. Kaplan, "Miami Grandma Targeted."

74. Stephanie DeGooyer, "Rethinking Birthright," *Boston Review*, July 18, 2019, http://bostonreview.net/law-justice/stephanie-degooyer-rethinking-birthright.

75. Wessler, "Is Denaturalization the Next Front in the Trump Administration's War on Immigration?"

76. Hilary Hurd Anyaso, "Hundreds of U.S. Citizens Continue to Be Detained, New Immigration Data Shows," Analysis Report, Northwestern University's Deportation Research Clinic, August 10, 2017, https://news.northwestern.edu/stories/2017/august/hundreds-of-u-s-citizens-continue-to-be-detained-new-immigration-data-shows/.

3. INVENTING ILLEGALITY

1. Adam Serwer, "White Nationalism's Deep American Roots," *Atlantic*, April 2019, https://www.theatlantic.com/magazine/archive/2019/04/adam-serwer-madison-grant-white-nationalism/583258/.

2. Jamie Ehrlich, "Rep. Duncan Hunter Posts Video Climbing over Fake 'Border Wall,' Opponent Claims He Violated Bail Agreement," CNN,

April 19, 2019, https://www.cnn.com/2019/04/19/politics/duncan-hunter
-border-video-violate-bail-agreement/index.html.

3. Kelly Lytle Hernandez, *Migra! A History of the US Border Patrol* (Berkeley: University of California Press, 2017), chapter 6.

4. Aristide R. Zolberg, *A Nation by Design: Immigration Policy in the Fashioning of America* (New York: Russell Sage Foundation, 2008), 253.

5. Mae M. Ngai, *Impossible Subjects: Illegal Aliens and the Making of Modern America* (Princeton, NJ: Princeton University Press, 2003), 26.

6. Serwer, "White Nationalism's Deep American Roots."

7. Serwer, "White Nationalism's Deep American Roots."

8. Serwer, "White Nationalism's Deep American Roots."

9. I am omitting the 1882 Chinese Exclusion Act even though it was nativist to the core, because it did not generate federal infrastructure for excluding and deporting. I take my cue here from the many historians who study US immigration, including Mae Ngai, S. Deborah Kang, and Kelly Lytle Hernandez.

10. Hidetaka Hirota, "The Stories of Irish Deportees from the US in 1800s," *Irish Times,* April 24, 2017, https://www.irishtimes.com/culture/books/the-stories-of-irish-deportees-from-the-us-in-1800s-1.3059578.

11. Greg Grandin, *The End of the Myth: From the Frontier to the Border Wall in the Mind of America* (New York: Metropolitan Books, Henry Holt and Company, 2019), 156.

12. Ngai, *Impossible Subjects,* 73.

13. Richard Alba and Victor Nee, *Remaking the American Mainstream: Assimilation and Contemporary Immigration* (Cambridge, MA: Harvard University Press, 2005).

14. Woodrow Wilson, *A History of the American People* (New York: Harper and Brothers, 1902), 98–99.

15. Don Wolfensberger, "Woodrow Wilson, Congress and Anti-Immigrant Sentiment in America: An Introductory Essay," Congress Project Seminar, "Congress and the Immigration Dilemma: Is a Solution in Sight?," Woodrow Wilson International Center for Scholars, March 12, 2007, https://www.wilsoncenter.org/sites/default/files/immigration-essay-intro.pdf.

16. Kevin M. Kruse, "Loaded Phrases: The Long, Entwined History of America First and the American Dream," *The Nation,* November 21, 2018, https://www.thenation.com/article/history-america-first-dream-sarah-churchwell/.

17. Henry Cabot Lodge, *Speeches and Addresses, 1884–1909* (n.p.: rarebooksclub.com, 2012).

18. Roger Daniels, *Guarding the Golden Door: American Immigration Policy and Immigrants Since 1882* (New York: Hill and Wang, 2005), 55.

19. Serwer, "White Nationalism's Deep American Roots."

20. Steve Willis, "Henry McCleary and the Land of the Rising Sun," *McCleary Museum Newsletter*, September 2001.

21. *Legalization of Residence of Certain Aliens: Report to Accompany H.R. 13795, Before the House of Representatives*, 70th Congress (1928) (report of Mr. Schneider, from the Committee on Immigration and Naturalization): "It should be explained that section 1 of the naturalization law of 1906 requires a registry to be made by the immigration authorities at the ports of entry of all aliens entering the United States on and after June 29, 1906. This provision, being part of the naturalization law, was overlooked by administrators of the immigration law for a number of years at the ports of entry into the United States from Canada."

22. This had been required by the 1906 Naturalization Act.

23. *Legalization of Residence of Certain Aliens: Report to Accompany H.R. 13795*.

24. S. Deborah Kang, *The INS on the Line: Making Immigration Law on the US-Mexico Border, 1917–1954* (New York: Oxford University Press, 2017), 41–43.

25. *Legalization of Residence of Certain Aliens: Report to Accompany H.R. 13795*.

26. Kang, *The INS on the Line*, 41–43: "the number of surreptitious entries into the United States was negligible."

27. Ngai, *Impossible Subjects*.

28. Kang, *The INS on the Line*, 21.

29. Kang, *The INS on the Line*, 16.

30. Kang, *The INS on the Line*, 12.

31. Kang, *The INS on the Line*, 20, 25.

32. Jeffrey S. Passel and D'Vera Cohn, "U.S. Unauthorized Immigrant Total Dips to Lowest Level in a Decade," Pew Research Center, November 27, 2018, https://www.pewhispanic.org/2018/11/27/u-s-unauthorized-immigrant-total-dips-to-lowest-level-in-a-decade/.

33. *Legalization of Residence of Certain Aliens: Report to Accompany H.R. 13795*, 4–5, quoting Fifteenth Annual Report of the Commissioner

General of Immigration, 1927: "So far as the manner of entry is concerned, an alien found unlawfully in the country for that reason or unable to prove his right to residence cannot be deported after five years. If not taken into custody during that period, he assumes the anomalous position of having the sanction of the law to remain but being barred from the right to citizenship. He is put in a still further embarrassing position should business or personal or family reasons dictate the necessity or desire to travel abroad.... This situation ... requires immediate remedial action. I cannot too strongly urge it upon the Congress. The legislation to accomplish it should take the form of a statute to give authority to the administrative officer to give legal domicile to aliens who entered the United States prior to July 1, 1924, the effective date of the present quota immigration law, upon showing in appropriate hearing that they are not subject to deportation on any other grounds and that they meet certain required standards."

34. Ngai, *Impossible Subjects*, 73.

35. *An Act Making it a felony with penalty for certain aliens to enter the United States of America under certain conditions in violation of law*, 70th Cong., 2nd Sess., Chapter 690 (1929), https://www.loc.gov/law/help /statutes-at-large/70th-congress/session-2/c70s2ch690.pdf.

36. See: *An Act Making it a felony with penalty for certain aliens*, 1929.

37. *A Bill to amend the immigration act of 1924*, 70th Cong., 1st Sess., H.R. 8540 (1928), 1928_3_27 hrg-1928-imn-0005_0002_from_51_to_100.

38. See: *A Bill to amend the immigration act of 1924*, pg. 38.

39. See: *A Bill to amend the immigration act of 1924*, pg. 38.

4. ENFORCING THE BORDER

1. Tanvi Misra, "Inside the Massive U.S. 'Border Zone,'" City Lab, May 14, 2018, https://www.citylab.com/equity/2018/05/who-lives-in-border -patrols-100-mile-zone-probably-you-mapped/558275/.

2. Suhauna Hussain, "How Trump's Wall Could Kill a Texas Border Town," Center for Public Integrity, October 9, 2018, https://apps.public integrity.org/abandoned-in-america/walled-off/.

3. Deborah Kang's excellent history of border policing highlights the fact that despite exclusions on Asian immigration, exceptions existed for merchants, especially at the southern border. S. Deborah Kang, *The INS on*

the Line: Making Immigration Law on the US-Mexico Border, 1917–1954, (New York: Oxford University Press, 2017), 25.

4. Greg Grandin, *The End of the Myth: From the Frontier to the Border Wall in the Mind of America* (New York: Metropolitan Books, Henry Holt and Company, 2019), 24.

5. Kelly Lytle Hernandez, *Migra! A History of the US Border Patrol* (Berkeley: University of California Press, 2017), 92–98, 145.

6. Kang, *The INS on the Line,* 42–43.

7. Rachel St. John, *Line in the Sand: A History of the Western U.S.-Mexico Border* (Princeton, NJ: Princeton University Press, 2011), 51.

8. Kang, *The INS on the Line,* 38.

9. Kang, *The INS on the Line,* 41–42.

10. Nicholas Villaneuva, *The Lynching of Mexicans in the Texas Borderlands* (Albuquerque: University of New Mexico Press, 2017).

11. Hernandez, *Migra!,* 37.

12. Kang, *The INS on the Line,* 25.

13. Hernandez, *Migra!,* 39.

14. Grandin, *The End of the Myth,* 21.

15. Kang, *The INS on the Line,* 48.

16. Kang, *The INS on the Line,* 48.

17. Kang, *The INS on the Line,* 50.

18. Kang, *The INS on the Line,* 70.

19. Kang, *The INS on the Line,* 72–73.

20. Kang quotes Wilmoth as seeking an "endless chain system": using each informant to find other suspects, who would then inform on yet more suspects. *The INS on the Line,* 116.

21. Kang, *The INS on the Line,* 116.

22. Quoted in Kang, *The INS on the Line,* 122.

23. Kang, *The INS on the Line,* 122–123.

24. See "An Act to amend the law relating to the authority of certain employees of the Immigration and Naturalization Service . . . ," 79th Cong., 2nd Sess., Chapter 768 (1946), https://www.loc.gov/law/help/statutes-at-large/79th-congress/session-2/c79s2ch769.pdf. It grants INS officers "power without warrant (1) to arrest . . . any alien who is in the United States in violation of any such law or regulation and is likely to escape before a warrant can be obtained for his arrest."

25. "Whenever in the opinion of a district director a distance in his district of more than 100 air miles from any external boundary of the United States would because of unusual circumstances be reasonable, such district director shall forward a complete report with respect to the matter to the Commissioner, who may . . . declare such distance to be reasonable." 8 C.F.R. § 287.1(b) (1957), https://cdn.loc.gov/service/ll/fedreg/fr022/fr022236/fr022236.pdf.

26. Kang, *The INS on the Line*, 116.

27. Hernandez, *Migra!*, 117.

28. Alex Wagner, "America's Forgotten History of Illegal Deportations," *Atlantic,* March 6, 2017, https://www.theatlantic.com/politics/archive/2017/03/americas-brutal-forgotten-history-of-illegal-deportations/517971/.

29. Hernandez, *Migra!*, 141.

30. Hernandez, *Migra!*, 206.

31. Wagner, "America's Forgotten History of Illegal Deportations."

32. This is the program known as 287(g).

33. Maeve Reston, "How Trump's Deportation Plan Failed 62 Years Ago," CNN Politics, January 19, 2016, https://edition.cnn.com/2016/01/19/politics/donald-trump-deportation-mexico-eisenhower/index.html.

34. Kang, *The INS on the Line.*

35. Hernandez, *Migra!*, 143.

36. Jim Newton, *Justice for All: Earl Warren and the Nation He Made* (New York: Riverhead Books, 2006), 136.

37. Although internment eventually ended, most Japanese Americans never recovered the farms, homes, property, businesses, and possessions that had been taken from them. In fact, even the farmland on which they had been incarcerated was eventually handed over to returning war veterans, a mostly white group. Robert Wilson, "Landscapes of Promise and Betrayal: Reclamation, Homesteading, and Japanese American Incarceration," *Annals of the Association of American Geographers* 101, no. 2 (February 18, 2011): 424–444, https://doi.org/10.1080/00045608.2010.545291.

38. H.R. 9980; Pub.L. 76-853; 54 Stat. 1137.

39. US Congress, House Committee on Immigration and Naturalization, Nationality Laws of the United States, committee print, 76th Cong., 1st Sess. (1939), 39–40.

40. Revision and Codification of the Nationality Laws of the United States, 76th Cong., 3d Sess. SR 2150 (1940).

5. TWO STEPS FORWARD

1. Daniel J. Tichenor, *Dividing Lines: The Politics of Immigration Control in America* (Princeton, NJ: Princeton University Press, 2009), 187–188.

2. Tichenor, *Dividing Lines*, 188.

3. Tichenor, *Dividing Lines*, 192.

4. Tichenor, *Dividing Lines*, 190.

5. Jack Wasserman, "The Immigration and Nationality Act of 1952: Our New Alien and Sedition Law," *Temple Law Quarterly* (1954): 80.

6. Tichenor, *Dividing Lines*, 192.

7. Tichenor, *Dividing Lines*, 192.

8. US Congress, Senate Committee on the Judiciary, Recording the Lawful Admission for Permanent Residence of Certain Aliens Who Entered the United States Prior to June 28th, 1940, report to accompany H.R. 11874, 85 Cong., 2 Sess., S.Rept. 85-1905, p. 2; US Congress, House Committee on the Judiciary, Recording the Lawful Admission for Permanent Residence of Certain Aliens Who Entered the United States Prior to June 28, 1940, report to accompany H.R. 11874, 85 Cong., 2 Sess., H.Rept. 85-1727, p. 2.

9. S.Rept. 85-1905, pp. 2–3; see also H.Rept. 85-1727, p. 2.

10. The law required that the alien not be legally considered "inadmissible" (ineligible for legal entry to the United States) under INA § 212(a) "insofar as it relates to criminals, procurers and other immoral persons, subversives, violators of the narcotics laws or smugglers of aliens." P.L. 85-616, August 8, 1958; 72 Stat. 546.

11. The letter stated that the bill's objective coincided with the "program of the President in respect to the conferral of discretionary authority upon the Attorney General to adjust the status of aliens in the United States who are found worthy of that privilege." S.Rept. 85-1905, pp. 2–3; see also H.Rept. 85-1727, p. 2.

12. The INA imposed caps on overall immigration from each hemisphere. The hemispheres' distinction has since been eliminated in favor of overall caps that allow residents of no country to receive more than 7 percent of visas in any given year.

13. Tom Gjelten, "Presidential Leadership: Uniting Behind Exceptionalism," *World Affairs* 179, no. 1 (June 2016): 119, doi:10.1177/0043820016662747.

14. Gjelten, "Presidential Leadership," 119, 120–121.

15. Muzaffar Chishti, Faye Hipsman, and Isabel Ball, "Fifty Years On, the 1965 Immigration and Nationality Act Continues to Reshape the United States," Migration Policy Institute, October 15, 2015, https://www.migrationpolicy.org/article/fifty-years-1965-immigration-and-nationality-act-continues-reshape-united-states.

16. Eventually *refuge* was removed from omnibus immigration legislation and treated as a distinct category. This reflects a long-standing distinction between people fleeing human rights abuses perpetrated or not prosecuted by their home-country governments and people fleeing other forms of suffering and emergency. Many who work in the field of human migration question the justifiability of this distinction, especially given that poverty is life-threatening for people trapped in failing economies.

17. The Immigration Bar here refers to the Association of Immigration and Nationality Lawyers. AINL (now AILA) is the nationwide professional association for immigration attorneys. Edward Dubroff was the person testifying on behalf of AINL. (He was a former president of AINL, and was at the time of his testimony the editor of its professional publication, the *Immigration Bar Bulletin*.) This was one submission that was delivered by one person on behalf of a national organization and with its blessing. The themes therein were echoed by others who testified before Congress to similar effect.

18. *Hearings Before the Judiciary Committee,* 88th Congress (August 5, 1964) (testimony of Mr. Dubroff) ("HRG1964HJH0009.pdf").

19. *Hearings Before the Judiciary Committee,* 88th Congress (1964) (testimony of Congressman Moore).

20. *Hearings Before the Judiciary Committee,* 88th Congress (June 11, 1964) (testimony of Congressman Fogarty, the sponsor of the bill to advance the registry date).

21. *Hearings Before the Judiciary Committee,* 88th Congress (June 11, 1964) (letter of President Lyndon Johnson to the Speaker of the House of Representatives, dated July 23, 1963).

22. *Hearings Before the Judiciary Committee,* 88th Congress (June 11, 1964) (testimony of Commissioner Farrell).

6. TWO STEPS BACK

1. César Cuauhtémoc García Hernández, "Immigration Detention as Punishment," *UCLA Law Review* 62, no. 5 (August 2013): 1360–1382, https://ssrn.com/abstract=2321219. Internal quote is from Jeff Yates et al., "A War on Drugs or a War on Immigrants? Expanding the Definition of 'Drug Trafficking' in Determining Aggravated Felon Status for Noncitizens," *Maryland Law Review* 64, no. 3 (2005).

2. Ruben Vives, "'I Left My Tacos on the Table and Took Off Running': Immigrants Remember the Workplace Raids of the 1980s," *Los Angeles Times*, January 14, 2017, https://www.latimes.com/local/california/la-me -immigration-trump-fears-20170109-story.html.

3. "Ku Klux Klan Plans Border Patrol to Help Fight Illegal Alien Problem," *New York Times*, October 18, 1977, https://www.nytimes.com /1977/10/18/archives/ku-klux-klan-plans-border-patrol-to-help-fight-illegal -alien.html.

4. Carly Goodman, "The Shadowy Network Shaping Trump's Anti-Immigration Policies," *Washington Post*, September 28, 2018, https://www .washingtonpost.com/outlook/2018/09/27/shadowy-network-shaping -trumps-anti-immigration-policies/?noredirect=on&utm_term= .9794d4a2db42.

5. Heidi Beirich, "John Tanton's Private Papers Expose More Than 20 Years of Hate," Southern Poverty Law Center, November 30, 2008, https://www.splcenter.org/fighting-hate/intelligence-report/2008/john -tanton's-private-papers-expose-more-20-years-hate.

6. John Tanton, "WITAN Memo III" to WITAN IV Attendees, October 10, 1986, private collection, https://www.splcenter.org/fighting-hate /intelligence-report/2015/witan-memo-iii.

7. Kathleen Belew, *Bring the War Home: The White Power Movement and Paramilitary America* (Cambridge, MA: Harvard University Press, 2018).

8. Heidi Beirich, "The Nativist Lobby: Three Faces of Intolerance," Southern Poverty Law Center, February 1, 2009, https://www.splcenter .org/20090131/nativist-lobby-three-faces-intolerance.

9. Beirich, "The Nativist Lobby."

10. Indeed, Tanton was the president of Northern Michigan Planned Parenthood from 1975 to 1978.

11. Quoted in Mario H. Lopez, "Hijacking Immigration?" Human Life Review, October 28, 2012, https://humanlifereview.com/hijacking-immigration/.

12. Jason DeParle, "The Anti-Immigration Crusader," *New York Times,* April 17, 2011, https://www.nytimes.com/2011/04/17/us/17immig.html.

13. This book is almost universally credited as a Sierra Club publication, but CIS indicates that they actually copublished with Sierra Club. Einat Sandman, *"What, Then, Is the American, This New Man?"* (Washington, DC: Center for Immigration Studies, 1998), https://cis.org/sites/cis.org/files/articles/1998/what.pdf.

14. Leon Bouvier, "Europe's Arab Future," *Social Contract* 16, no. 3 (Spring 2006), https://www.thesocialcontract.com/artman2/publish/tsc1603/article_1392.shtml.

15. Leon F. Bouvier, *Peaceful Invasions: Immigration and Changing America* (Lanham, MD: University Press of America, 1992).

16. Southern Poverty Law Center, "Extremist Files: Federation for American Immigration Reform," Accessed July 17, 2019, https://www.splcenter.org/fighting-hate/extremist-files/group/federation-american-immigration-reform.

17. I learned this in an email exchange with Carly Goodman, which is on file with the author along with copies of the original documents. Carly Goodman, email exchange with author, March 23, 2019.

18. Dylann Roof credits the CCC with spurring his radicalization. David A. Graham, "The White-Supremacist Group That Inspired a Racist Manifesto," June 22, 2015, *Atlantic,* https://www.theatlantic.com/politics/archive/2015/06/council-of-conservative-citizens-dylann-roof/396467/.

19. Southern Poverty Law Center, "Extremist Files: Council of Conservative Citizens," accessed July 17, 2019, https://www.splcenter.org/fighting-hate/extremist-files/group/council-conservative-citizens.

20. Southern Poverty Law Center, "Extremist Files: Council of Conservative Citizens."

21. Council of Conservative Citizens, "Conservative Headlines," updated January 31, 2017, http://conservative-headlines.com/introduction/statement-of-principles/.

22. Southern Poverty Law Center, "Extremist Files: Council of Conservative Citizens."

23. Francis edited the CCC's newsletter. Southern Poverty Law Center, "Extremist Files: Sam Francis," accessed July 15, 2019, https://www.splcenter.org/fighting-hate/extremist-files/individual/sam-francis.

24. Stephen Piggott, "FAIR Digs Up 20 Year Old Video Series Borderline, an Anti-Immigrant TV Series That Gave Platforms to Numerous White Nationalists," Southern Poverty Law Center, April 20, 2017, https://www.splcenter.org/hatewatch/2017/04/20/fair-digs-20-year-old-video-series-borderline-anti-immigrant-tv-series-gave-platforms.

25. Piggott, "FAIR Digs Up 20 Year Old Video Series Borderline."

26. Richard D. Lamm, "It's Time to Look at Who We Are Admitting, Not Just How Many," Center for Immigration Studies, March 1, 2001, https://cis.org/Report/Its-Time-Look-Who-We-Are-Admitting-Not-Just-How-Many.

27. Southern Poverty Law Center, "Extremist Files: Garrett Hardin," accessed July 17, 2019, https://www.splcenter.org/fighting-hate/extremist-files/individual/garrett-hardin.

28. Jane Coaston, "Peter Brimelow and VDare, the White Nationalist Website with Close Ties to the Right, Explained," Vox, September 24, 2018, https://www.vox.com/2018/8/22/17768296/peter-brimelow-vdare-kudlow-white-house-racism.

29. Southern Poverty Law Center, "Extremist Files: VDARE," accessed July 17, 2019, https://www.splcenter.org/fighting-hate/extremist-files/group/vdare.

30. Peter Brimelow, *Alien Nation: Common Sense About America's Immigration Disaster* (New York: Random House, 1995).

31. Samuel P. Huntington, *Who Are We? The Challenges to America's National Identity* (New York: Simon and Schuster, 2005).

32. Jonathan Blitzer, "The Border Patrol Was Primed for President Trump," *New Yorker,* February 17, 2017, https://www.newyorker.com/news/news-desk/the-border-patrol-was-primed-for-president-trump.

33. *Hearings Before the Judiciary Committee,* 97th Congress (1982) (testimony of Mr. Rudd, Congressman of the United States).

34. *Hearings Before the Judiciary Committee,* October 9, 1986 (testimony of Congressman Daub) ("CR19861009PL99603H.pdf"). See also testimony of Congressman McCollum ("For those who have been here since January 1, 1976, even by adopting my amendment to strike legalization, they will be able to stay if the Attorney General says so under his discretion, because we have moved up the registry date from 1948 to 1976. I think that is appropriate"). One of the proposals for advancing registry pinned the date to 1976, but the date ultimately adopted was 1972.

35. Immigration Control and Legalization Amendments Act of 1985: H.R. 580, 99th Cong. (1986).

36. Center for Immigration Studies, "New Immigration and Naturalization Services Report," October 12, 2000, https://cis.org/New-INS-Report.

37. David Simcox, "The Cost of the IRCA Amnesty After 10 Years: Measuring the Fallout," Center for Immigration Studies, May 1, 1997, https://cis.org/Report/Cost-IRCA-Amnesty-After-10-Years.

38. Alison Siskin, "Noncitizen Eligibility for Federal Public Assistance: Policy Overview," Congressional Research Service Report, RL33809, December 12, 2016, https://fas.org/sgp/crs/misc/RL33809.pdf.

39. Office of the Assistant Secretary for Planning and Evaluation, "Overview of Immigrants' Eligibility for SNAP, TANF, Medicaid, and CHIP," US Department of Health and Human Services, March 27, 2012, https://aspe.hhs.gov/basic-report/overview-immigrants-eligibility-snap-tanf-medicaid-and-chip.

40. Alex Nowrasteh and Robert Orr, "Immigration and the Welfare State: Immigrant and Native Use Rates and Benefit Levels for Means-Tested Welfare and Entitlement Programs," Cato Institute, May 20, 2018, https://www.cato.org/publications/immigration-research-policy-brief/immigration-welfare-state-immigrant-native-use-rates.

41. Alyce P. Miller, "From Immigrants to Activists: Immigration, Nativism, Welfare Reform and the Mobilization of Immigrant Voters in the Late Nineteenth and Late Twentieth Centuries," PhD diss., University of North Carolina, 2012, http://libres.uncg.edu/ir/uncg/f/Miller_uncg_0154D_11046.pdf. See especially page 20 ("Through efforts by politicians such as Ronald Reagan, anti-immigrant activists such as John Tanton, and anti-immigrant interest groups such as FAIR, the hierarchical structures of the undeserving poor [or 'welfare queen,' as popularized by Ronald Reagan in the 1970s and 1980s] and that of the immigrant as a drain on society and governmental resources converged in the mid-1990s"); page 23 ("In the 1990s, articles in the *National Review* began to blast the INA for what it saw as the INA's role in not only increasing the numbers of immigrants, but in ensuring that almost all of these immigrants lacked 'useful' skills, were poor, and were from third world countries"); and page 25 ("Republican California State Assemblyman William J. Knight circulated throughout the state legislature a racist poem given to him by a constituent, 'Everything is mucho good. / Soon we own the neighborhood / We have a hobby—it's called breeding. / Welfare Pay for baby feeding.' This poem typified some of the racist rhetoric in support of Proposition 187, which combined antiwelfare and

anti-immigration symbols. Proposition 187 made all government services, including public education, inaccessible to illegal aliens. It also mandated reporting of suspected illegal immigrants by schools, teachers, doctors, etc. Proposition 187 did not come from the fringe of immigration discourse. In fact, it largely echoed the recommendations of the United States Commission on Immigration Reform [CIR]").

42. CRS Report for Congress, "Border Security: The San Diego Fence," May 23, 2007, https://fas.org/sgp/crs/homesec/RS22026.pdf.

43. Alan Greenblatt, "Buchanan Hopes His Vote Will Give Him a Voice," *Congressional Quarterly,* May 20, 1995 (quoting Buchanan as saying, "It's outrageous that American taxpayers, as hard-pressed as they are . . . have to provide social welfare benefits for those whose accomplishments are to break the laws to get into the United States and to get on welfare").

44. Carly Goodman, "Angry That ICE Is Ripping Families Apart? Don't Just Blame Trump. Blame Clinton, Bush, and Obama, Too," *Washington Post,* June 11, 2018, https://www.washingtonpost.com/news/made-by-history/wp/2018/06/11/angry-that-ice-is-ripping-families-apart-dont-just-blame-trump-blame-clinton-bush-and-obama-too/?utm_term=.138124ba9288.

45. Janice Kephart, "Immigration and Terrorism: Moving Beyond the 9/11 Staff Report on Terrorist Travel," Center for Immigration Studies, September 1, 2005, https://cis.org/Immigration-and-Terrorism.

46. Steven A. Camarota, "The Open Door: How Militant Islamic Terrorists Entered and Remained in the United States, 1993–2001," Center for Immigration Studies, May 1, 2002, https://cis.org/Report/How-Militant-Islamic-Terrorists-Entered-and-Remained-United-States.

47. Alex Nowrasteh, "Terrorism and Immigration: A Risk Analysis," Cato Institute, September 13, 2016, https://www.cato.org/publications/policy-analysis/terrorism-immigration-risk-analysis#full.

48. Bill Hing, "The Racism and Immorality of the Operation Gatekeeper Death Trap," *Border Criminologies* (blog of the University of Oxford Faculty of Law), April 13, 2015, https://www.law.ox.ac.uk/research-subject-groups/centre-criminology/centreborder-criminologies/blog/2015/04/racism-and.

49. The services had been provided by the government-funded Legal Services Corporation (LSC). It was a circumscribed program, to be sure, but the 1996 restrictions on LSC assistance to noncitizens was part of a dramatic systematic attack on the rights of noncitizens in the United States.

50. Human Rights Watch, "Deportation Law Based on Criminal Convictions After 1996," report, July 2007, https://www.hrw.org/reports/2007/us0707/5.

51. American Immigration Council, "Aggravated Felonies: An Overview," December 16, 2016, https://www.americanimmigrationcouncil.org/research/aggravated-felonies-overview.

52. "Immigration Consequences of Delinquency and Crimes," report by Kids in Need of Defense, 2017, https://supportkind.org/wp-content/uploads/2015/04/Chapter-10-Immigration-Consequences-of-Delinquency-and-Crimes.pdf.

53. American Immigration Council, "Aggravated Felonies: An Overview."

54. Teresa A. Miller, "Citizenship and Severity: Recent Immigration Reforms and the New Penology," *Georgetown Immigration Law Journal* 17 (2003): 611–666, https://digitalcommons.law.buffalo.edu/articles/408/.

55. Carl Shusterman, "BIA Defines Hardship Standard for Cancellation of Removal," Immigration Daily, 2001, https://www.ilw.com/articles/2001,0614-Shusterman.shtm.

56. "Forced Apart (By the Numbers): Non-Citizens Deported Mostly for Nonviolent Offenses," Human Rights Watch, April 15, 2009, https://www.hrw.org/report/2009/04/15/forced-apart-numbers/non-citizens-deported-mostly-nonviolent-offenses.

57. "Forced Apart (By the Numbers): Non-Citizens Deported Mostly for Nonviolent Offenses."

58. P.L. 104–208, Div. C, 10 Stat. 3009.

59. P.L. 104–208, Div. C, 10 Stat. 3009 at § 102(a).

60. These bills variously proposed to change the registry date to January 1, 1982 (H.R. 3149), January 1, 1984 (S. 1552), and January 1, 1986 (H.R. 4138, H.R. 4172, H.R. 4200, S. 2407, S. 3068, S. 3095). In addition to establishing a new registry date of 1986 upon enactment, S. 2407, S. 3068, and S. 3095 would have instituted a "rolling registry date" system to advance the registry date in one-year increments in each of the five years from 2002 to 2006. These annual adjustments would have continued until January 1, 2006, when the registry date would have advanced from January 1, 1990, to January 1, 1991.

61. Jeffrey Passel, "New Estimates of the Undocumented Population in the United States," Migration Policy Institute, May 22, 2002, https://www.migrationpolicy.org/article/new-estimates-undocumented-population-united-states.

7. NERVOUS BREAKDOWN

1. Gallup News, "In Depth: Topics A to Z, Immigration," accessed June 24, 2019, https://news.gallup.com/poll/1660/immigration.aspx.

2. Steven A. Camarota, "The Open Door: How Militant Islamic Terrorists Entered and Remained in the United States, 1993–2001," Center for Immigration Studies, May 1, 2002, https://cis.org/Report/How-Militant -Islamic-Terrorists-Entered-and-Remained-United-States.

3. "9/11 Terrorist Attacks," Center for Immigration Studies, July 7, 2019, https://cis.org/Immigration-Topic/911-Terrorist-Attacks?type =All&page=0.

4. Camarota, "The Open Door."

5. David Seminara, "Hello, I Love You, Won't You Tell Me Your Name: Inside the Green Card Marriage Phenomenon," Center for Immigration Studies, November 30, 2008, https://cis.org/Report/Hello-I-Love-You-Wont -You-Tell-Me-Your-Name-Inside-Green-Card-Marriage-Phenomenon.

6. "Bank of America Boycott," Americans for Legal Immigration PAC (ALIPAC), sponsored by the National Illegal Immigration Boycott Coalition NIIBC, updated June 24, 2019, http://www.bankofamericaboycott .com/americans_for_legal_immigration/.

7. Americans for Legal Immigration PAC, "ALIPAC Platform," accessed June 24, 2019, https://www.alipac.us/ourplatform/.

8. Miranda Blue, "ALIPAC's Tasteful 9/11 Message: 'Illegals Are Hijacking Our Government: Let's Roll Americans,'" Right Wing Watch, September 11, 2013, http://www.rightwingwatch.org/post/alipacs -tasteful-911-message-illegals-are-hijacking-our-government-lets-roll -americans/.

9. President George W. Bush, Executive Order 13228, Section 2, October 8, 2001.

10. David Rittgers, "Commentary: Abolish the Department of Homeland Security" (originally published in *Washington Times,* September 19, 2011), CATO Institute, https://www.cato.org/publications/commentary /abolish-department-homeland-security.

11. Elizabeth C. Borja, "Brief Documentary History of the Department of Homeland Security, 2001–2008," Department of Homeland Security History Office, 2008, https://www.hsdl.org/?view&did=37027.

12. The reorganization entailed transferring twenty-two agencies from Agriculture, Defense, Energy, FBI, GSA, HHS, Justice, and other

departments to the newly formed DHS. These included FEMA, Coast Guard, Secret Service, INS, the US Customs Service, Federal Protective Service, various infrastructure and energy grid–related agencies, biological inspections agencies, and more.

13. Functions such as those performed by Treasury's Customs Inspection unit, certain intelligence investigation units, etc., were added to the CBP and ICE portfolio despite not coming from INS.

14. Additionally, certain agencies were transferred in whole or in part to the Department of Justice, such as the Bureau of Alcohol, Tobacco, and Firearms (from Treasury).

15. Miriam Jordan, "Wait Times for Citizenship Have Doubled in the Last Two Years," New York Times, February 21, 2019, https://www.nytimes.com/2019/02/21/us/immigrant-citizenship-naturalization.html.

16. George W. Bush, "Securing the Homeland, Strengthening the Nation," https://www.dhs.gov/sites/default/files/publications/homeland_security_book.pdf.

17. See, e.g., Department of Homeland Security, "Budget in Brief: Fiscal Year 2005," https://www.dhs.gov/dhs-budget-brief-fiscal-year-2005.

18. See, e.g., Department of Homeland Security, "Budget in Brief: Fiscal Year 2010," https://www.dhs.gov/sites/default/files/publications/budget_bib_fy2010.pdf.

19. See, e.g., Department of Homeland Security, "Budget in Brief: Fiscal Year 2016," https://www.dhs.gov/sites/default/files/publications/FY_2016_DHS_Budget_in_Brief.pdf.

20. Also included were Securing Cyberspace, Aviation Security, American Preparedness and Resilience (referring to FEMA work), and Protecting the Nation's Highest Leaders and Safeguarding Financial Infrastructure. See, e.g., Department of Homeland Security, "Budget in Brief: Fiscal Year 2018," https://www.dhs.gov/sites/default/files/publications/DHS%20FY18%20BIB%20Final.pdf.

21. Bush, "Securing the Homeland, Strengthening the Nation."

22. Department of Homeland Security, "U.S. Department of Homeland Security Annual Performance Report: Fiscal Years 2011–2013," Department of Homeland Security, accessed July 26, 2019, p. 66, https://www.dhs.gov/sites/default/files/publications/dhs-congressional-budget-justification-fy2013.pdf.

23. Department of Homeland Security, "Budget Overview: Congressional Justification Fiscal Year 2019," US Immigration and Customs Enforcement, 2019, O&S-54; O&S-92, https://www.dhs.gov/sites/default/files /publications/U.S.%20Immigration%20and%20Customs%20Enforcement .pdf.

24. Department of Homeland Security, "Budget Overview: Congressional Justification Fiscal Year 2019."

25. Department of Homeland Security, "Budget Overview: Congressional Justification Fiscal Year 2019," O&S-54; O&S-92.

26. Department of Homeland Security, "Budget Overview: Congressional Justification Fiscal Year 2019," 54. Interestingly, before the Trump administration, there was a fourth programmatic component: the Visa Security Program (VSP). See Department of Homeland Security, "Congressional Budget Justification FY 2017," US Immigration and Customs Enforcement, 90, https://www.dhs.gov/sites/default/files/publications /FY2017CongressionalBudgetJustification-Volume2.pdf. It appears that VSP's work was absorbed into International Operations.

27. Italics are mine. See Department of Homeland Security, "Budget Overview: Congressional Justification Fiscal Year 2019," 62.

28. Department of Homeland Security, "Budget Overview: Congressional Justification Fiscal Year 2019," 76.

29. Department of Homeland Security, "Budget Overview: Congressional Justification Fiscal Year 2019," 85.

30. Jimmy Tobias, "Exclusive: ICE Has Kept Tabs on 'Anti-Trump' Protesters in New York City," *The Nation*, March 6, 2019, https://www.thenation .com/article/ice-immigration-protest-spreadsheet-tracking/.

31. Ryan Devereaux, "Homeland Security Used a Private Intelligence Firm to Monitor Family Separation Protests," The Intercept, April 29, 2019, https://theintercept.com/2019/04/29/family-separation-protests -surveillance/.

32. Department of Homeland Security, US Immigration and Customs Enforcement, "Budget Overview: Congressional Justification Fiscal Year 2019," 92, https://www.dhs.gov/sites/default/files/publications/U.S.% 20Immigration%20and%20Customs%20Enforcement.pdf.

33. Department of Homeland Security, US Immigration and Customs Enforcement, "Budget Overview: Congressional Justification Fiscal Year 2019," 92.

34. Department of Homeland Security, US Immigration and Customs Enforcement, "Budget Overview: Congressional Justification Fiscal Year 2019," 114–115.

35. Department of Homeland Security, US Immigration and Customs Enforcement, "Budget Overview: Congressional Justification Fiscal Year 2019," 115.

36. Franklin Foer, "How Trump Radicalized ICE," *Atlantic,* September 2018, https://www.theatlantic.com/magazine/archive/2018/09/trump-ice/565772/.

37. Alice Speri, "Internal Emails Show ICE Agents Struggling to Substantiate Trump's Lies About Immigrants," The Intercept, October 4, 2017, https://theintercept.com/2017/10/04/ice-raids-trump-immigration-deportation/.

38. "The Cost of Immigration Enforcement and Border Security," American Immigration Council Special Report, January 25, 2017, https://www.americanimmigrationcouncil.org/research/the-cost-of-immigration-enforcement-and-border-security.

39. Congressional Research Service, "Comparing DHS Component Funding, FY 2019: In Brief," Congressional Research Service, July 9, 2019, 2, https://fas.org/sgp/crs/homesec/R45262.pdf.

40. Eileen Sullivan, "Obama Administration to End Use of Private Prisons," *PBS NewsHour,* August 18, 2016, https://www.pbs.org/newshour/nation/obama-administration-end-use-private-prisons.

41. Notably, in FY2017, ICE requested only $2.2 billion for detention. However, the DHS appropriations act provided $2.6 billion, explaining that "for the past several years, the agency's forecast for the required number of detention beds and its cost estimates have resulted in budget requests that missed the mark by wide margins." See Explanatory Statement, 163 Cong. Rec. H3327, H3811 (daily ed. May 3, 2017), accompanying the Department of Homeland Security Appropriations Act, 2017, Pub. L. No. 115-31, https://www.gao.gov/assets/700/691330.pdf, and United States Government Accountability Office, "Immigration Detention: Opportunities Exist to Improve Cost Estimates," Report to Congressional Committees, April 2018, https://www.gao.gov/assets/700/691330.pdf.

42. Many states have reverted from private-contract incarceration to public facilities because the private facilities were so costly. "Private Prison Population Skyrockets," Equal Justice Initiative, August 8, 2018, https://eji.org/news/private-prison-population-skyrockets.

43. Homeland Security Advisory Council, "Report of the Subcommittee on Privatized Immigration Detention Facilities," Immigrant Justice, December 1, 2016, https://www.immigrantjustice.org/sites/default/files /content-type/press-release/documents/2016-12/DHS_HSAC_PIDF_Report -FINAL_DRAFT.pdf. This figure includes the revenues of BI Incorporated since its acquisition by GEO in 2011.

44. Revenue source figures come from here: CoreCivic, *2017 Annual Report*, 2017, p. 2, "Financial Highlights," http://ir.corecivic.com /static-files/097a67c7-bd56-442d-aa48-99f2ac87e3a4.

45. Department of Homeland Security Office of Inspector General, "Immigration and Customs Enforcement Did Not Follow Federal Procurement Guidelines When Contracting for Detention Services," February 21, 2018, https://www.oig.dhs.gov/sites/default/files/assets/2018-02 /OIG-18-53-Feb18.pdf.

46. See Department of Homeland Security, US Immigration and Customs Enforcement, "Budget Overview: Congressional Justification Fiscal Year 2018," ICE budget report, https://www.dhs.gov/sites/default/files/publications /ICE%20FY18%20Budget.pdf; and Department of Homeland Security, US Immigration and Customs Enforcement, "Budget Overview: Congressional Justification Fiscal Year 2019," https://www.dhs.gov/sites/default/files /publications/U.S.%20Immigration%20and%20Customs%20Enforcement .pdf; and Department of Homeland Security, "Budget Overview: Congressional Justification Fiscal Year 2017, Volume II, US Immigration and Customs Enforcement, Transportation Security Administration, U.S. Coast Guard," https://www.dhs.gov/sites/default/files/publications/FY%202017%20 Congressional%20Budget%20Justification%20-%20Volume%202_1.pdf.

47. Livia Luan, "Profiting from Enforcement: The Role of Private Prisons in U.S. Immigration Detention," Migration Policy Institute, May 2, 2018, https://www.migrationpolicy.org/article/profiting-enforcement-role -private-prisons-us-immigration-detention.

48. Luan, "Profiting from Enforcement."

49. Luan, "Profiting from Enforcement."

CONCLUSION

1. Mike Lillis, "GOP's New Immigration Weapon," *The Hill*, May 16, 2014, https://thehill.com/homenews/house/206281-released-criminals -become-gops-new-weapon-in-immigration-fight.

2. Andorra Bruno, "Immigration: Registry as Means of Obtaining Lawful Permanent Residence," CRS Report for Congress, August 22, 2001, http://congressionalresearch.com/RL30578/document.php.

3. Bruno, "Immigration."

4. Jeffrey S. Passel and D'Vera Cohn, "Unauthorized Immigrant Population Stable for Half a Decade," Pew Research Center, September 21, 2016, https://www.pewresearch.org/fact-tank/2016/09/21/unauthorized-immigrant-population-stable-for-half-a-decade/.

5. Jeffrey M. Jones, "In U.S., 65% Favor Path to Citizenship for Illegal Immigrants," Gallup News, August 12, 2015, https://news.gallup.com/poll/184577/favor-path-citizenship-illegal-immigrants.aspx.

6. Robert Lynch and Patrick Oakford, "The Economic Effects of Granting Legal Status and Citizenship to Undocumented Immigrants," Center for American Progress, March 20, 2013, https://www.americanprogress.org/issues/immigration/reports/2013/03/20/57351/the-economic-effects-of-granting-legal-status-and-citizenship-to-undocumented-immigrants/.

7. Lynch and Oakford, "The Economic Effects of Granting Legal Status and Citizenship to Undocumented Immigrants."

8. GAO audited DHS in 2011 and recommended developing a systematic approach to immigrant incorporation because there was none in place. United States Government Accountability Office, "Immigration Integration: U.S. Citizenship and Immigration Services Could Better Assess Its Grant Program," Report to the Ranking Member, Committee on Homeland Security, House of Representatives, December 2011, https://www.gao.gov/assets/590/587090.pdf.

9. Julie Veroff, "Asylum Officers Are Being Replaced by CBP Agents," American Civil Liberties Union, May 6, 2019, https://www.aclu.org/blog/immigrants-rights/ice-and-border-patrol-abuses/asylum-officers-are-being-replaced-cbp-agents.

10. Anna O. Law (@UnlawfulEntries), "Working on cleaning data, but here's a first cut at our objective variables in our Immigration Judge dataset," Twitter, July 17, 2019, 9:01 a.m., https://twitter.com/UnlawfulEntries/status/1151522214207881223.

Index

USCIS (United States Citizenship
and Immigration Services), 10,
38, 71–72, 74, 175, 199
use-of-force policies, 35
US-Mexico border, enforcement
along, 7–8. *See also* Border
Patrol; border wall

VDARE, 152
vehicle stops, CBP jurisdiction and,
48–49
"vice squads," 111–113
video hearings, 64
video translation, 64
visas
lack of established system for,
94–95
overstaying, 98
short-term work, 97–98

Walter, Francis, 129
War Relocation Authority, 121
warrants, 48–49, 113
Warren, Earl, 122
Wartime Measure Act (1918), 95
Watson, Davino, 67
weapons, military-grade, 32–34
welfare benefits, 159–160
Weyrich, Paul, 152
White Citizens' Councils, 150

white nationalism/racism
in 1990s, 186
civilian groups and, 23–24
family reunification and, 134
Hart-Celler bill and, 132–133
"illegal" immigration and,
84–86
National Origins Act and, 91–94,
100
paramilitary organizations and,
15–16
scientific racism, 89–90
Tanton's work and, 145–153
Tea Party and, 79
whiteness, definitions of, 85–86
Williams, Lee, 98
Wilmoth, Grover C., 115–116
Wilson, Woodrow, 91
WITAN memos, 150
work requirements, 164
work speedups, 62–63
work visas, short-term, 97–98
World Trade Center bombing
(1993), 161–162, 186
World War II, 71, 121–122, 128

Yousef, Ramzi, 162

Zero Population Growth, 146
Zero Tolerance program, 34–35, 60

SUSAN KAHN

ELIZABETH F. COHEN is professor of political science at the Maxwell School of Citizenship and Public Affairs at Syracuse University and the author of *The Political Value of Time*. She lives in New York City.